THE JACKBOOTS

ROBYN ROBINS

The Jackboots
Copyright © 2025 Robyn Robins
All rights reserved.
Print ISBN: 978-1-7638845-2-6
Ebook ISBN: 978-0-6450394-9-8
Published by A Sense of Place Publishing 2025

Reviewers and editors may use up to 500 words of this book with attribution. Any larger extracts or other usage should be negotiated with the publisher.

Otherwise no parts of this publication may be reproduced, stored in a retrieval system, or transmitted in any form or by any means, electronic, mechanical, photocopying, recording, or otherwise, without the prior written permission of the copyright owner or the publisher.

This book is sold subject to the condition that it shall not, by way of trade or otherwise, be lent, resold, hired out, or otherwise circulated without the publisher's prior consent in any form of binding or cover other than that in which it is published and without a similar condition including this condition being imposed on the subsequent purchaser. Under no circumstances may any part of this book be photocopied for resale.

Cover design by Jessica Bell
Editor John Stapleton

 A catalogue record for this book is available from the National Library of Australia

To Mum

And to those who also leave behind threads of light to be taken up by the children of the future who will weave a new blanket of light, love and peace

CONTENTS

GRATITUDE 9
AUTHOR'S INTRODUCTION 15

PART 1 A PIVOTAL TIME IN HISTORY 19
   FREEDOM FIGHTERS. 21
   PEACEFUL WARRIORS 35
   MEDICAL MUTINY 43
   AUSTRALIAN HEALTH PROFESSIONALS SPEAK OUT. . . . 47
   WHY AUSTRALIA REMAINS
   A PENAL COLONY FOR PHYSICIANS 55
   NZDSOS. 59
   THE PATH OF COURAGE 61
   THE GRAND JURY THE COURT OF PUBLIC OPINION. . . . 69
   SHOW US THE VIRUS. 77

PART 2 OUR SOULS ARE BEING CORRUPTED 81
   WHITE ROSE. 83
   DO NOT LET ANYONE TOUCH YOUR KIDS 89
   WHERE ARE THE OLD TO LISTEN? 105
   "WHEN THE GRANDMOTHERS SPEAK
   AND ARE LISTENED TO THE WORLD
   WILL BEGIN TO HEAL" 111
   THE FARMERS' REVOLUTION. 117

PART 3 CREATING A NEW WORLD . . . . **.129**
LIFE WITHOUT FEAR. 131
A RETURN OF THE SOPHIA 137
THE BEST VACCINE EVER INVENTED 143
AUTHOR'S MUSINGS 161
EPILOGUE 163
A RIVER OF TEARS 183

PART 4 RELATED BOOKS,
DOCUMENTARIES AND WEBSITES . . . . **.187**
THE LION SLEEPS NO MORE 189
WEBSITES 191
BOOKS/DOCUMENTARIES. 207
AUTHOR'S STORY. 223
REFERENCE LIST 227
BIBLIOGRAPHY 251

GRATITUDE

"With the broken promise of 'Never Again', we picked up the thread of the past and find ourselves barrelling down the path of destruction that will come to not only harm the whole of humanity but to all things creeping and crawling, green and unfurling organic for the entire life. Those of us bearing witness to the changes across the globe do so with gratitude for having the eyes to see the changes taking place. That gratitude comes equally with the obligation to do all within the resources of our thoughts, actions and will to see the continuation of creation and the human species 1.0."
Ilana Rachel Daniel,
The Grand Jury the Court of Public Opinion, 2022

I have endeavoured to write from integrity.

The information I have referenced, I believe to be from a source with similar values, however, this may not always be the case. I have included reference material so that you may carry out your own research and use your own discretion. However, due to the dynamic nature of the internet, web addresses or links contained in this book may no longer be valid.

I do not dispense medical advice or prescribe the use of any technique as a form of treatment for physical, emotional or medical problems without the advice of a physician. My intent is to only offer information of a general nature.

The Jackboots are coming
Darkness is on the march
The Jackboots have no feeling
They taser, bash and bully
Are cruel, heartless and soulless
Dark clouds are coming
There will be no place to hide
From radiation tanks contaminating the waterways
While the ocean weeps bitter tears
Who will stop the Jackboots
From weaving a quilt of destruction
Who will save the children
From the false world created by mindless media
Movies of horror, games of violence
From injections that poison and change the DNA
From toxic chemicals that darken the soul
Who will see the children's tears
Hear their cries when chemtrails spray death
Who will grow food to feed their soul
Awaken them to smell the roses
For the rose is a celestial being of light
Within the rose is forgotten wisdom
A gateway through the dark
Who will awaken and smell the roses
Who will stop the Jackboots

Robyn Robins – September, 2012

To the shining lights, these writings mention a small number of you but there arc many. Those who tirelessly marched and protested, refused to wear masks, social distance or to take an experimental procedure, I refer to as the Covid-19 jab.

To the Truckers who led a protest that became a worldwide event – turning the tide.

THE JACKBOOTS

To the health care professionals who spoke truth despite the threats and the censorship. Many left their employment rather than adhere to the mandates and others were stripped of credentials depriving their communities of much needed expertise. Under duress, some followed the mandates so they could continue to do what they do best, support those in need.

To the legal community who tirelessly worked to seek retribution and acknowledgement for the many lives lost, for the jobs and businesses lost and as-a-consequence, the ability to care for family and to halt the mandating of vaccines, especially for children.

To the law enforcement who spoke out against the encroaching tyranny. Some turned a 'blind eye' to businesses who defied the mandates, those who did not mask, nor kept the social distance rules. Many were forced to leave their profession due to illegal mandates and underhanded tactics.

To the businesses who welcomed all, vaccinated and unvaccinated and risked the wrath of the Jackboots to uphold their integrity.

To those who risked retribution to keep the people informed and who against all odds, kept on keeping on. To the journalists who gave the people a platform from which to speak their truth and tell their stories.

To the musicians and artists who bravely sent a message of support to the people despite the censorship imposed on their industry.

To the farmers and those who maintained the food chain despite the many obstacles. You are the backbone of your country.

To the mums and dads who worked day in and day out to give the children a-safe-haven, taking the blows as they came and expanded their hearts to shield the young. Never was the job of parenting so challenged.

To the Rainbow Warriors, foretold in the prophecies that this would be your time to reclaim the Earth and all its creatures from the domination of dark forces. Some say that we did not choose to be here at this auspicious time, we were chosen.

To everyone who showed up. We are the ones we were waiting for and the time is now.

My gratitude to John Stapleton and A Sense of Place Publishing for your courage, support and expertise.

I feel blessed for having experienced the sisterhood, women who have worn many garbs, felt the winds blowing in their hair and the sun shining on their face. Women who have survived the trials of fire, earth, air and water, have walked the hot coals, and, still, one appears at your side when your world is cold and alone. Thank you to those who walk the corridors of time passing the flame of sisterhood through the generations. May your light shine. Today, like no other, the young need your wise counsel for they too weave and spin their dreams, hopes and wishes. They too will need your gentle support when their home is cold and they are alone. Thank you from my heart dear sisters.

My personal gratitude to the sisterhood for supporting me to bring this book to completion.

My gratitude to my two proof-readers for witnessing the rocky road taken when writing this book, whose love, support and brilliance held my wobbly heart.

My gratitude to the friends who stepped forward with their varied healing gifts, ongoing love and support.

I feel blessed for having experienced the love of family and to be reminded that years of caring and sharing too are a spiritual currency that can return with interest when most needed.

My Earth Angel grandchildren for wrapping me within your wings during my darkest hours and always.

My gratitude to warrior nephews and nieces who stepped forward with support when the dark curtain fell.

To my precious boys, you have given me more love and support than I could have ever hoped.

My gratitude to my wonderful team of doctors and practitioners for the years of 'true medicine' without which I would not have been in a healthy position to complete this work.

"One has a moral responsibility to disobey unjust laws."
Martin Luther King

"Disobedience becomes a sacred duty when the State becomes lawless or corrupt."
Gandhi

"Those who deny freedom to others, deserve it not for themselves."
Abraham Lincoln

"Silence in the face of evil is itself evil: God will not hold us guiltless. Not to speak is to speak. Not to act is to act."
Dietrich Bonhoeffer – German Lutheran pastor and part of the German resistance movement against Nazism

"The truth is like a Lion. You don't have to defend it. Let it loose. It will defend itself."
Saint Augustine, the doctor of the Roman Catholic Church

"There is no medicine for your morals. If your morals are gone, you go."
Eddie Jaku – 2020

AUTHOR'S INTRODUCTION

"I tell ye true, liberty is the best of all things.
Never live beneath the noose of a servile halter."
William Wallace, 1270 – 1305

A lone man walked up the steps of Parliament House in Canberra. A line of faceless police barred his entry. An overweight policeman carrying a machine gun slinked out of the shadows.

This was the year 2022.

And then, men emerged from the crowd of many who had converged on the Capital of Australia, in trucks, cars, on bikes, on foot, and leapt to the defence of the lone man. Everyone heard the shouts, "Shoot me!" "No, shoot me, I am old."

The man with the machine gun retreated.

David had unflinchingly faced Goliath, thrown down the gauntlet and the silent war on humanity fought in the dark recesses of unsuspecting minds was no longer hidden. After two long years of enduring a global agenda carried out in a lockstep of horror, the people of Earth were awakening. A terror had been released on an entire planet but worldwide, people were unmasking and saying, 'No'. The spirit of humanity is alive and well.

As in any war, there are usually two sides, the 'goodies' and the 'baddies'– the light and the dark. Some are saying that we are fighting a spiritual war. The first step to winning any war, is to become aware that you are in one. Many are becoming aware that it has been playing out in the shadows of everyday life for a long time. Many are still asleep and others, having closed their eyes and said 'goodnight' to one world, awakened in another reality.

"Who is the enemy?" these sleepy ones might ask.

"I thought the enemy was a virus," some might ponder.

After the realisation that we are in a war, the next step is to know the opponent's identity. Could a virus be so powerful that it turned the world upside down almost overnight, threatening the very existence of humanity as we know it? A virus renowned scientists are saying has yet to be proven to exist.

The global rich and famous, known as the Global Elite, are the face of the Giant who holds within its grasp powerful players such as the Rockefellers and the Rothschilds, George Soros, Klaus Schwab and Bill Gates. The Giant's controlling hands reach into the banking, the medical, the religious and the scientific institutions, the judiciary and the education systems.

The Giant has a controlling influence in investment corporations such as Black Rock, Vanguard and State Street that have ownership stakes in companies that influence every corner of our lives. According to Michael Navradakis' research, Black Rock with more than $9.5 trillion in assets as of July 2021 and Vanguard holding more than $7 trillion in assets as of January 2021, are among the top three shareholders of the Covid vaccine makers Pfizer, Moderna and Johnson and Johnson. Their tentacles reach into humanity's societal structure to own, control and educate.

The Giant has captured the industrial military complex and its arsenal of weaponry including 5th generation warfare tactics such as bioweapons made in laboratories, weather weaponisation technology, electromagnetic radiation technology and the manipulation of food supplies. The Giant's plans were put into place and implemented over a long period of time. A psychological warfare that began long ago has been unleashed upon humanity using weaponry such as desensitisation, degradation of integrity and the creation of a perpetual state of fear and chaos have proven to be effective in bringing about submissive acceptance.

The Giant has captured the worldwide media and censors the voices offering an opinion that is contrary to its agenda. Many are unaware pawns carrying out the Giant's agenda and others have been coerced by blackmail, bribery and threats to self and family.

The United Nations and underpinning organisations such as the World Health Organisation (WHO), the International Monetary Fund (IMF), the Intergovernmental Panel on Climate Change (IPCC), the World Trade Organisation (WTO) and the World Bank are the Giant's voice and take policies to those who enforce its' commands. These bodies include governments worldwide, the scientific and medical establishments and others who sew the threads into a carefully woven matrix designed to enslave all beings on Planet Earth.

A master magician, the Giant has placed a whole planet under its spell.

The Giant's agenda, however, is being revealed. Klaus Schwab, Founder and Executive Chairman of the World Economic Forum has publicly talked about the Great Reset, the Fourth Industrial Revolution, a plan to redistribute resources to the Global Elite. He said, "You will own nothing and you will be happy." The world population will live under digital surveillance, twenty-four hours per day – humanity's biological and digital identities will be fused. In his July 2020 book, *Covid-19 and The Great Reset*, this agenda is discussed. However, he said that the greatest threat to this becoming a reality is the freedom loving people of Earth.

In 2021, Chile's President, Sebastian Pinera, said that the best way to predict the future is to invent it and that is what they aspire to achieve.

Humanity's rights and freedoms are being taken away with each day that passes and you may ask: "If, We The People, are represented by the biblical David carrying five small stones and a slingshot and many are still sleeping, how can we triumph over such a powerful force?"

Ah! The sleepy ones are waking up, taking up spiritual swords and joining the fight for what is most precious to humanity, freedom. They fight for the safety of the children and the future they will inherit. They fight to honour the spirit of the ancestors and the legacy they have left and they fight for the Earth and its inhabitants from the mineral, plant and animal kingdoms. They fight for a future where all peoples live in a free society, equally supported, cherished and loved. They fight for the right to create a space of love where children will be nurtured and grow into their full potential through having the capacity to express empathy, sympathy, kindness, warmth and love.

A united humanity will triumph and then, the little man hiding in the shadows with a machine gun, symbolic of the Giant, will disappear, its arsenal of terror will be no more.

PART 1
A PIVOTAL TIME IN HISTORY

"These are the times that try men's souls. The summer soldier and the sunshine patriot will, in this crisis, shrink from the service of their country – but he that stands by it now, deserves the love and thanks of man and woman. Tyranny, like hell, is not easily conquered – yet we have this consolation with us, that the harder the conflict, the more glorious the triumph. What we obtain too cheap, we esteem too lightly: it is dearness only that gives everything its value. Heaven knows how to put a proper price upon its goods – and it would be strange indeed if so celestial an article as FREEDOM should not be highly rated."
Thomas Paine, 13 December, 1776

FREEDOM FIGHTERS

"Thank you for fighting for my future."
The Children

"Rallies are vast in their effectiveness. When people come together in one united voice of love and care for humanity and a right to freedom, they change the world."
Sandy Stevenson

"Thank you for fighting for my future" – "Go convoy go".

These messages from the children were written in ink on packages of food donated to the convoy that had travelled to Canberra, Australia, where a real-time drama played out that would affect the lives of every man, woman and child.

Chefs set up tents to cater for everyone and food, including organic vegetables and fruit, began to arrive.

"How much love" was a comment heard.

Danny from the Sunshine Coast drove fifteen hours to reach his destination and said, "I can't sit at home anymore and look my children in the eyes. We love this country and want to save it for our children. Some people have forgotten their spirit and now is the time to get it back – I know you have it (Editor, *Cairns News*, 2022)."

On that historic weekend, 12-13 February, 2022 despite efforts to block technology, 'alternative news' outlets were successful in getting information to the people. Hardly a word was heard from the mainstream media except to downplay the rally, its significance and to vilify the peaceful protesters. All the while, reporting on the latest manufactured scandal, the 'movie' designed to capture the attention of the masses.

The Canadian Freedom Convoy that converged on the country's capital to 'take back their country' had been the spearhead of this movement. Truckers from many countries took up the gauntlet. Reported to be more than fifty thousand, the Canadian convoy travelled from the country's far-reaches to gather in Ottawa on 29 January, 2022 and vowed to remain until all Federal mandates were removed. Along the way, masses of people cheered the heroes and provided food and supplies. In return, it was said that the Truckers cleaned streets, shovelled snow and fed the homeless.

The atmosphere wherever the warriors went was one of 'it's party time'. Dancing, music, singing, laughter and fun filled the streets. Jumping castles were set up for the children, ice hockey became a favourite pastime. Humanity was coming together under the banner of freedom, unity and love. Warriors from every walk of life, race, colour and creed united to bring love back into the world.

Placards told the story:

"Freedom over Fear"

"Love over hate"

And, the whole human race was now different.

The Prime Minister, Justin Trudeau moved out of his residence saying that he was going into quarantine, having been in contact with Covid. The government threatened fines and imprisonment, and lawyers stepped up to support those fighting for freedom. Blockades emerged on main transport routes and on border towns such as on the road to Coutts, said to have been lined with protestors for approximately twenty miles in support of the Truckers. This blocked access to the Canada-USA border crossing.

The Emergency Act of 1988 was invoked, giving the government special powers. It could order banks to freeze or suspend bank accounts without a court order and with protection from civil liability. The Editor of *Cairns News*, reported that this did happen to truckers and some who supported them through donations. It said that a GoFundMe account that had raised approximately ten million dollars to support the Truckers was cancelled and the funds were to be redirected to 'approved charities'. This did not happen and the monies were returned to the original donors.

Mike Adams, known as The Health Ranger said, "What Canada, Trudeau and TD Bank are demonstrating here for the entire world to see is that we can't trust the financial institutions anymore, since they will collude with criminal governments to steal money from innocent people.

"In other words, the entire Covid 'plandemic' caused people to lose all faith in Big Pharma, government regulators, science journals and the media. Now, through these acts of financial terrorism, Canada and TD Bank are giving people new reasons to abandon any remaining faith in mainstream financial institutions."

It was into the third week of peaceful protests that the Jackboots (a symbol for totalitarianism) were sent to disperse the growing crowd of freedom fighters. Official badging was not to be seen on a proportion of this militarised force. Black uniforms attacked the people with pepper spray, water cannons, lasers and batons. The war horse trampled and traumatised, arrests were made, pets confiscated and vehicles smashed.

Trudeau backed down saying that the Emergency Act had been put in place to 'protect the people' but he was confident the law-and-order authorities were capable of handling this situation. Could the massive run on the banks to withdraw money have been a more likely reason? Time will tell the story and it will depend on who 'wins' the war, how this is told.

American truckers launched The Peoples' Convoy on 23 February, 2022 from Adelanto Stadium in Southern California to Washington DC to join the call to Freedom led by the Canadian truckers. They said, "We are the people of the United States of America and we stand together under the banner of freedom – freedom is the one thing that unites us all. Liberty flows through all of our veins (Transcriber B)."

Rebel News reported that in New Zealand, hundreds of protesters camped outside of the Parliament for approximately four weeks refusing to leave until their demands were met. When the Jackboots, decked out in 'war costumes', were sent to forcibly remove the peaceful crowds, violence broke out and people on both sides were injured. The Jackboots used their weaponry to combat the peaceful warriors who were saying no to facing unemployment, being locked out of society unless submitting to the mandates and being coerced into participating in a clinical trial with no long-term safety data.

"Shame on you," were the unified cries from those who once thought of the police as their friend and ally. "Shame on you," they chanted.

The Walk of Shame will be the fate of many.

David Hawkins MD, PhD developed the Map of Consciousness and said, power unifies and serves others, whereas force is self-servicing. Violence is force and true power needs no validation.

The freedom fighters had unleashed a power within the human psyche that those seeking self-interest, could not understand. The Giant in its ignorance and arrogance had underestimated the gentle David. The war was not won, but the battle had succeeded in bringing humanity together and revealed for everyone to see was the face of an inhumane opponent.

Many were becoming aware that to concede to the Giant's demands would not result in a return to 'normal'. Coming into consciousness was the realisation that the Covid-19 story had been bubbling away under the surface for a long time. In 2017 hundreds of millions of Covid-19 test kits were ordered for world distribution (Sorenson, 2021). And, then Event 201, a Pandemic Simulation Exercise, on how a coronavirus pandemic would play out world-wide, was held in New York on 19 October, 2019. Sponsored by the Gates Foundation, the World Economic Forum and the John Hopkins Center for Public Security, this became the peoples' reality when in December 2019, the official announcement of a new and potentially 'deadly' coronavirus was announced.

Unleashed upon the world in lockstep were horrors such as PCR testing, mandated mask wearing, social distancing and lockdown.

In response to the 'pandemic' and under an Emergency Use Authorisation (EUA), the Covid-19 jab was then released. Although no long-term safety studies were shown, the mantra that it was 'safe and effective' became the reassurance that a panacea had been miraculously found.

Two pathways were emerging. One leading to the New World Order, a transhuman society in which humanity would become a part of the 'Internet of Things', the 'Internet of Bodies' – Klaus Schwab's Fourth Industrial Revolution. The threat from the World Economic Forum saying "It is 2030 and you own nothing and you will be happy," would become the reality.

The 'yellow brick road' was revealed for all to see. Dorothy in the *Wizard of Oz* took this pathway and it led to the 'man behind the curtain'. This is where we are at now. The question is, "Will we remain under the spell of the 'man behind the curtain' and continue on the pathway to a world of transhumanism?" Or, "Will we become aware that we have the power to ensure the rights to our own body, to informed consent, parental rights, freedom of speech and the right to travel and trade within a potpourri of human potential?" This pathway is our second choice.

Jeffrey Prather (retired Special Operations Soldier, former DIA Intelligence Collector, and ex-DEA Special Agent) believes we are in global World War Four, the Human Resistance against the Global Elite tyranny. The vectors are big pharma, big medicine, big science, big everything but the Global Resistance fighting for life and freedom for all beings is building.

The tip of the spear, he said, is Canada.

World War III is recognised by many as being the War on Terror when rights were slowly eroded and surveillance crept into every aspect of our lives. Meanwhile, in Australia, Lurnpa (also known as David Cole) of the Luritja Wombai people sent a video message to the Australian people outlining what he believed to be the agenda behind the unfolding medical tyranny. An excerpt from this powerful speech said:

> *"This is a once-in-a-lifetime opportunity for us to stand together – black and white – to unite, to take back our*

country and to stop this genocide against all people. And to keep the land healthy, to keep the land safe for future generations.

"We can do this. We can work together. We just have to unite and stand together as one.

"Please, work with us. Let's stand together. Let's free us.

"Freedom and power to humanity."

On that weekend in February 2022, an astounding number of people showed up to demand the end of mandates and to dissolve Parliament. It was the largest rally in Australia's history. According to the police estimate, 1.4 million vehicles arrived up to Friday and the drone count was reported to be 2.4 million people. The Editor, *Cairns News* (2022) reported Ricardo Bossi's (author, speaker, Senate Candidate, Former Army Special Forces, Lieutenant Colonel and National leader of Australia One Party) thank you speech to the people of Australia.

He said,

> *"The love, the happiness the joy was brilliant and millions and millions of us said that it is time they backed off. We communicated to the powers to be that we have had enough and presented our demands: the Governor General present himself, dissolves Parliament, appoint an executive council giving them three months to clean up the electoral process and then have the first free and fair election within sixty years. It was a fantastic party atmosphere, we must come together as one people, one country, one flag."*

If the Parliament is acting unconstitutionally, the Governor General is required to warn, he is required to dissolve and he is required to appoint. And, Australians were waking up to the fact that the country's corporate government is not constitutional.

The formal list of demands also included bringing an end to vaccine mandates and passports and to acquire informed parental consent for children – to end the state of emergency in all states and repeal the Victorian pandemic bill – open state borders and investigate Covid-19 misconduct with a Royal Commission with the power to prosecute.

No sitting Member for Parliament appeared to address the people. The Prime Minister played the ukulele on television and the propaganda campaign for the upcoming election was well under way to divert the attention of the people. He declared that the Commonwealth Government could not impose mandates and 'passed the buck' to the States. The opposition leader sent a message to the protesters to say, "Go home" and not a peep was to be heard from the Governor General.

They did the unforgivable by releasing long range acoustic and electromagnetic weapons on the men, women and children protesting in love for peace and freedom. This vicious attack caused an array of distressing symptoms including chemical burns, nausea and pounding headaches. The Jackboots, decked out in 'war costumes' were armed, masked and wore ear plugs. It was reported that one Jackboot had a spare set around his neck and when asked to give it to a distressed child, the request was ignored. They interfered with the private communication devices belonging to the people.

The Jackboots had previously shown that they are no friend to the people and now they could be liable under Section 28 of the Federal Crimes Act 1914. This states in brief: "Any person who, by violence or by threats or intimidation of any kind, hinders or interferes with the free exercise or performance, by any other person, of any political right or duty, shall be guilty of an offence. Penalty: imprisonment for 3 years."

The right to assemble is a basic human right.

A lady who attended the rally described the energy as being uplifting, supportive and loving, and the number of people who made the journey was fantastic. Especially, she commented, when considering that for everyone present, there would have been at least one other person supporting their protest.

She explained that when making the commitment to travel to Canberra, friends and family came forward with money, camping gear and tyres for her car. They expressed gratitude to her for doing this for them. Her protest also enfolded those she had worked with, the handicapped people in whom she had witnessed a decline in health after receiving Covid-19 jabs. She protested the loss of her job due to mandates.

We The People are witness to the crimes being carried out against humanity and this, we must not forget, however, we must become aware that crimes are being committed. Sadly, it seems true for many that personal lives need to be threatened before a stand is taken.

I grew up in the post-war era surrounded by male family and friends who considered it to be their job to care for those they loved and to make every effort to create a life benefiting the society in which they were a part. This was the generation that had survived dark years of conflict, had experienced times of little food, little money and often, little hope.

When writing about the Second World War, my mum in her memoir, called *Wonderful Kindred Spirits* written for family and friends, said, "We lost so many friends, our youth was wiped away and overnight, we grew up. Boys went away and came back men with a different look on life."

I remember her talking about the chokos! Hunger was real, especially during the Great Depression and she wrote: "I hate those rotten chokos – those green water blobs. The neighbours kept us supplied and my mum baked them in a tin, put pink cochineal in the sago and so we had 'pink pears a la sago boiled naturelle'. I now know why we were always suffering boils and styes on our eyes. We had malnutrition."

The story of her mum saying that she had eaten or was not hungry is part of the family tapestry. Mum wrote: "I often wondered why my parents, especially Mum, had said she had eaten earlier. I know now that my brother and I needed to be fed and my dad had to have his strength to tramp for miles looking for work. Mum went without and she was thin."

Fear and hunger are traumas and if not resolved can be stored in vibrational patterns within the body. Until the day Mum left her home to go into care, she kept a small amount of cash hidden in the house and a cupboard of imperishable food consisting of two tins of a variety of food that were never to be touched. The fact that they were out of date did not seem to occur to her, or perhaps did not matter.

However, she also wrote, "I do not know how to describe the terrific feeling of togetherness, helping and loving and the comradeship. I believe it will never come again."

I must have experienced an echo of that when growing up because I remember a felt sense of being cocooned in strength and protectiveness. 'The men of steel' a friend once said in her remembrance.

In my latter years, I have wondered, "Where is the fire in the belly?"

And, over the past two years, "Where is the Australian spirit?"

The Australian spirit over many generations has become clouded by the deliberate attempt by the Giant and its 'merrymen' to disconnect the people from the spirit of humanity. However, I believe we are seeing the fire in the soul beginning to shine.

The 'men of steel' are emerging and at the same time, the dark forces are increasing their bullying tactics which at the end of the day, is all they have. When Toto in the *Wizard of Oz* drew back the curtain, revealed was a frightened little man and that is what we are now seeing. Albeit, one with deadly toys and because of the crimes committed that are now being brought into the open, one that has nothing to lose.

Del Bigtree told Dr Patrick Gentempo in 2021, "That is the most dangerous opponent you can have. These people now have nothing to lose. They know that they're dead if they don't win and so they're going to fight to the death. That's where we are at. We're at that place now in this world that those that are against us have bought in so hard and lied so much that they cannot win a case in a courtroom and certainly not in the court of public opinion." He said that although the force against the people is so huge that it looks like we simply cannot win, we will. History is full of examples of the David and Goliath story.

Dell Bigtree reminded us, "That story has been written in our blood throughout history and I really do believe we are blessed to be a part of a generation that is going to write that history again."

Dr Patrick Gentempo, a chiropractor, author and co-founder of *Revealed Films* with Jeff Hays asked himself where the beauty is in all of this. He said, "The beauty is the people who are standing up, waking up and doing something, taking action that is heroic in nature which is the full expression of the human spirit."

Meanwhile, vaccine adverse event reporting systems (the CDC's VAERS, the United Kingdom's Yellow Card System, the European EUDRAVigilance System, Australia's Adverse Event Monitoring System and the WHO's VigiAccess Database) were revealing an alarming increase in deaths and injuries from the Covid-19 jab. This, despite data to show that cases recorded through these systems are far lower than the actual cases in the real world.

According to a government funded Harvard Pilgrim Health Care study, the United States of America VAERS system (Vaccine Adverse Effects Reporting System) revealed reported data to be potentially as low as one percent. There are many reasons for this including the fact that medical practitioners are taught to deny the existence of injury, are afraid of the consequences if they do lodge a report, many do not know the system exists and those that do, find it a long and complicated process.

For example, the July 2021 release from the VAERS database showed nearly seven thousand reported deaths associated with the SARS-coV-2 vaccines. This number is more than the total number of vaccine deaths reported in the preceding fifteen years. When considering that professionals who speak out against the Covid story are now being persecuted, this underreported data is sobering.

Dr Stephanie Seneff, a senior research scientist at MIT, studied issues relating to human health for over a decade. Her degrees from MIT, one of the most prestigious science and tech universities in the world, are in biology, electrical engineering, and computer science. She spoke at the World Council For Health on 3 January, 2021 re her published paper with Dr Greg Nigh reviewing some, but not all, of the concerns that they were aware of in relation to the SARS-coV-2 vaccine.

These included pathogenic priming, allergic reactions, Antibody Dependent Enhancement (ADE) and activation of latent viral infections.

Neuro-degenerative disease was reviewed and Dr Seneff said, "We would see increased rates of Parkinson's disease and in people getting it younger and younger into the future and not necessarily connecting it to the vaccine."

The paper concluded that finally, as an obvious but tragically ignored suggestion, the government should be encouraging the population to take safe and affordable steps to boost their immune systems naturally. These included getting out in the sunlight to raise vitamin D levels (Ali, 2020) and eating mainly organic whole foods rather than chemical-laden processed foods (Rico-Campà et al, 2019).

Eating foods that are good sources of vitamin A, vitamin C and vitamin K2 should be encouraged, as deficiencies in these vitamins are linked to bad outcomes from Covid-19 (Goddek, 2020; Sarohan, 2020).

Dr Seneff reminded us to get out in the sun without sunscreens that often contain dangerous chemicals and block elements of sunlight that are important for our bodily function. She said that the rising rates of melanoma skin cancer has been going up exactly in step with the rise in use of sunscreen. We have, in fact, an epidemic of Vitamin D deficiency along with this aggressive use of sunscreen (Rich The Renegade, 2022).

However, guidance from health officials to take safe and effective health measures was not being encouraged and despite the mounting evidence that the Covid-19 jabs were causing death and disability, the rollout continued. It was becoming apparent that until we knew what we were dealing with, it was important to protect our bodies.

Nonetheless, a breakthrough did occur when due to the efforts of United States attorney Aaron Siri and his team, Pfizer was mandated on 6 January, 2022 by Judge Mark T Pittman under Court Orders to release 55,000 pages per month relating to the Pfizer BioNTech Covid vaccine approval process. This transpired despite Pfizer asking for 75 years to disclose claiming limited resources, the need to protect personal information and to protect trade secret interests.

Naomi Wolf, an author at *DailyClout,* called for volunteers to come forward to sieve through the thousands of pages. Approximately 3500 doctors, lawyers, scientists, data analysts and others responded. Dr Chris Flowers, physician, radiologist and breast cancer specialist came out of retirement to take up the lead.

Epidemiologists showed that there was no spike in the number of deaths in 2020 and funeral directors testified that this is correct. United Kingdom Funeral Director, John O'Looney when being interviewed by Dr Reiner Fuellmich (2021) said that this is indeed the story. In 2020 there were no excess deaths, however, he said the reality is that the death rate only soared when they began putting needles in arms in January 2021.

John O'Looney took The Road Less Travelled and was suspended from the Society of Allied and Independent Funeral Directors (SAIF) for his courageous interviews revealing a powerful insight into the Covid story.

Those working in the medical field could not help but witness the death and injury caused by the Covid-19 jab. Among the medical professionals who stayed within the system, there are those who abandoned their ethics and morals by obeying the Giant's 'merrymen'.

A friend, coerced into receiving the jab against her will to keep her job, became ill the night of having the procedure. The following day, she reported to her general practitioner what was happening only to be told that it was 'normal'. She was curtly offered an MRI to seek an explanation for the terrible headaches she experienced, which she refused. And then, was offered another 'safe and effective' jab.

Another friend who also took the jab against her will to keep her business going, said that she felt like she had been raped. She told me that others she had spoken to had felt the same way. Indeed, this is medical rape, vicious and cruel and to compound the wounding, cushioned on betrayal that can cripple the life.

Dr Christiane Northrup said, "This is a raping of your cells and a forced genetic experiment without Informed Consent of the trial participants and thus violates Nuremberg Codes. Humanity has a duty to shut down Big Pharma's genocide experiment immediately (Love, 2021)."

Mandated and forced vaccination does not allow for informed consent as set out in the Nuremberg Code No 1: Voluntary Consent is Essential.

It is time to stand up and make choices that will lead to freedom.

If we lose the right to determine what goes into our body, then we have lost freedom. What may follow could be a very dark existence for our children and their children because we will have lost the ability to protect them.

PEACEFUL WARRIORS

"If you know the enemy and know yourself, you need not fear the result of a hundred battles. If you know yourself but not the enemy, for every victory gained you will also suffer a defeat. If you know neither the enemy nor yourself, you will succumb in every battle."
Sun Tzu – 496 BC-544 BC

"Warriors confront the evil that most people refuse to acknowledge."
Bohdi Sanders, 2014

The years 2020 – 2022 on Planet Earth were dark and chaotic, cycles ending and beginning, prophecies and conspiracy theories coming true. Dark winds swept away a civilisation almost overnight. Many had no idea what was happening. Fear gripped the hearts of the masses, rendering them inert.

However, there were those who had sensed the coming apocalyptic times and their warnings had infiltrated into everyday society. Others wrote books on the dark foundations on which the planet was wobbling. There were some who gave their lives and endured hardships to infiltrate and gain an understanding of the darker side.

As a practising yoga teacher for many years, my passion for health and wellbeing led me to explore alternative pathways when receiving a breast cancer diagnosis in 2012. It was during that time the work of investigative journalist, filmmaker and humanitarian Jonathan Otto came to my attention. At the beginning of the Covid story when my soul was saddened by what I thought to be a dimming of the human spirit, Jonathan Otto's first documentary was released. I then knew that his bringing together the voices of warriors from many different walks of life would gain momentum. It has and there have been documentaries to follow. His passion and dedication have been a cornerstone to the Health Freedom Movement.

"Follow your heart, this is God speaking," was Dr Rashid Buttar's advice to Jonathan Otto when contemplating beginning the Covid series. Jonathan Otto did and so must we.

The growing number of freedom fighters stand on the shoulders of the warriors who relentlessly held the line. Perhaps there is no better way to tell this story than through the words of a small portion of those whom we were fortunate enough to hear speak and this, I have attempted to do throughout the pages of these writings. The following peaceful warriors were among the first to raise their voice in protest to the official story that was unfolding during those turbulent years. They raised concerns regarding the SARS-coV-2 injections and brought awareness to artificial intelligence technology that had been covertly introduced into our everyday lives.

Jonathan Otto said, "Where were you when the world went down in flames? This is a fight. We have to stand for each other. Love and God will prevail."

DR RASHID A BUTTAR

Dr Rashid Buttar, an osteopathic physician, served as Brigade Surgeon and Director of Emergency Medicine while in the United States army. Board certified in clinical metal toxicology, preventive medicine, board eligible in emergency medicine, Dr Buttar achieved fellowship status in three separate medical societies.

In an interview with Jonathan Otto (Vaccine Secrets: Reloaded, 2021), Dr Buttar summarised his protocol for maintaining good health and to prevent becoming susceptible to any pathogen. He said that good nutrition, rest and exercise are key. Become aware of areas of toxicities underlying ill health: heavy metal toxicity, persistent organic pollutants (such as being exposed to harmful chemicals) and glyphosate. Opportunists (such as bacteria, cycoplasma, yeast), microwaves, electromagnetic frequencies and emotional and psychological toxicity are areas to explore. Food (not what we are eating but what we do to food such as homogenisation, pasteurisation, genetic modification and irradiation) and spiritual toxicity are important.

Dr Buttar said: "The jab rewrites the code that makes us human and how we respond to our environment. We are destroying the innate immune system."

Dr Buttar mentioned glyphosate and through the work of Dr Stephanie Seneff and Dr Anthony Samsel, we learned of its role in many health issues. They linked glyphosate to autism and it has been found in nearly all vaccines, the MMR containing the highest levels.

See Dr Seneff's book, *Toxic Legacy*.

DR BRIAN HOOKER

Dr Brian Hooker, a Professor of Biology at Simpson University in California, specialising in microbiology and biotechnology, is the Children's Health Defense Chief Scientific Officer.

When speaking of aborted foetal cells, Dr Hooker told Jonathan Otto (Vaccine Secrets: Reloaded, 2021) that most vaccines are derived from or tested on human foetal tissue. He believed this to be a huge issue for not only vaccines but also food preparations (colourings and flavourings) and medicines where these are used.

Dr Hooker said: "All life is sacred and our bodies do not know what to do with this foreign matter."

Sayer Ji, the Founder of GreenMedInfo, the world's most widely referenced, evidence-based natural health resource of its kind and co-founder of Stand for Health Freedom, agreed.

Sayer Ji said (Otto, Vaccine Secrets, 2021): "Karma is involved in the inhuman acts needed to create these technologies. Rudolf Steiner said that the world will produce a vaccine to inject darkness into the human soul. Is this a way to dislocate children from their own souls?"

DR ANDREW KAUFMAN

Dr Andrew Kaufman MD, a forensic psychiatrist and molecular biologist, received his training and degrees from Duke University, MIT and South Carolina Medical University. He is a founding member of the World Doctors Alliance and a producer of the documentary, *Terrain*.

When interviewed by Laura-Lynn Tyler Thompson (2021), Dr Kaufman said that no virus has been shown to exist and no experimental evidence of a new disease. We only have diagnostic tests that have never been approved and have never undergone a basic validation study. He said that this is a psychological operation generating vast amounts of fear through mainstream media and giving false information to create a delusion. He explained that when people are in this state of fear and panic, they are more easily conditioned to follow instructions from authority. The delusion that there is some dangerous new illness that you must change your life and give up freedoms to overcome, is not based on science but on propaganda.

Dr Kaufman said: "If we do not make a stand to this tyranny, it will be more and more difficult. Take the path of courage."

DR CARRIE MADEJ

Dr Carrie Madej received her medical degree from Kansas City University of Medical Biosciences in 2001. She practised osteopathic and internal medicine and is now an educator in human rights and nanotechnology.

Dr Madej was one of the first to talk about artificial intelligence technology – hydra, nanobots, graphene-like particles and structures that self-assemble once introduced through the vaccine. She said that part of the World Economic Forum's agenda to link every human on the planet to the Internet of Things or the Internet of Bodies (to become a wireless device), is openly discussed and is to be implemented by 2030.

In 2021, Professor Dr Pablo Campra, University of Almeria, Spain, was the first to discover graphene oxide in the Pfizer, Astrazeneca, Moderna and Janssen Covid vaccines. Other prominent scientists followed (laquintacolumna.net).

The Vaccine Death Report revealing scientific evidence that millions have died and hundreds of millions have suffered crippling side effects was written by David John Sorensen and Dr Vladimir Zelenko MD. It stated: "Graphene oxide is the perfect conductor for 5G, and the best substance for brain manipulation. The Chilean president said that 5G will insert thoughts and feelings into everyone. Klaus Schwab says that humanity will be lifted into one and the same consciousness. This reveals an agenda of total mind control."

In June 2022, Dr Madej and her partner miraculously escaped death when their light plane crashed for no apparent reason. She told Mike Adams, the Health Ranger that at the heart of the incident, she remembered God telling her many years ago that she would not die in a plane crash.

Dr Madej said: "And I'm fearless now. I'm not afraid of death. Not at all! And when you lose that fear, you finally start living again and you just say, 'No!'…"

DR VLADIMIR ZELENKO

Dr Zelenko, a board-certified physician, practised in New York and was a Nobel Peace Prize nominee.

In an interview with Jonathan Otto (Covid Secrets Reloaded, 2022) he said: "There is a twenty-year patent trail that describes the development of a weapon of mass destruction called Covid-19. There is nothing natural about it, it was modified in stages over twenty years and then deployed on humanity."

Dr David E Martin PhD, the founding CEO of M-Cam received his undergraduate from Goshen College, a Masters of Science from Ball State University and his Doctorate from The University of Virginia. He told Dr Patrick Gentempto (2021) that what we are calling SARS-coV-2 today is a CDC patent plus published modifications. His team tracked over four thousand, one hundred patents specific to the treatment, detection and vaccination of SARS-coV-2 lodged during the period 23 April, 2003 to the birth of SARS-coV-2 in December 2019. Four thousand, one hundred different people, organisations, institutions, companies, etc. lodged patents that had a common link back to the funding sources.

Dr Zelenko explained that we are dealing with a device that can deliver a technology into seven billion people. It is patented and there are fifty pages of complex data that describes this technology that is already in the vaccines. It allows for the measurement of temperature, blood pressure, etc. and transmits that data to a third party with your location. Another patent describes the linking of biometric data to cryptocurrency. What is happening in China is going to be happening globally – the central banks outlawed all crypto currency, issued a digital yuan and linked this to a social score system. You must have that technology in you to participate in society.

Dr Zelenko said: "This is the mechanics of global enslavement. The only solution is to say 'No', take kids out of school and build cities of refuge."

On 30 June, 2022 Dr Vladimir 'Zev' Zelenko passed away.

"Today our dear friend and a true Hero of Humanity Dr Vladimir Zelenko has left his earthly body, and was taken up into the glorious realms, from where he will continue his fight for a better future of humanity. Your voice will become louder than ever," said David Sorensen from the website *Stop World Control*.

Dr Zelenko spoke of his cancer diagnosis as a gift from God, preparing him to withstand persecution and ridicule. He said that he had looked death in the eye and feared nothing on this Earth. Dr Zelenko fought for his life and at the same time, fought for humanity. He received regular death threats and was censored on Twitter, Facebook, and just about everywhere they could censor him. He created the Zelenko Freedom Foundation, dedicated to continuing his work.

When interviewing him on *The HighWire*, Dell Bigtree thanked him for having the courage and the vision to stand up for others. Dr Zelenko replied that he wanted to leave a good legacy for his children, "To do what's right and not what's easy. I would rather sacrifice my present and have a future than sacrifice my future for a few conveniences in the present."

He said: "I have the only protocol and that is to use common sense and keep people alive."

My dad used to shake his head and say, "There's no nouse," meaning there is little common sense. He believed all the book learning in the world was useless without a bit of nouse thrown in. Claire Nahmad (2008) tells us that nouse represents the mind within the heart, the connection between soul and spirit, the wisdom we use to ride the waves whilst surfing in the great sea of life and the vision within the soul. By learning to go within, the natural breath can take us to a place of peace where the gift of nouse may be granted and we may find the inner physician who knows the true meaning of the words, 'First, do no harm'.

In December 2022, The Zelenko Foundation honoured six 'Worthy Women' in the Health Freedom Movement with the Rosa Parks Award. These were: Maureen McDonnell, Sherri Tenpenny, Christiane Northrup, Judy Mikovits, Carrie Madej and Barbara Lo Fisher.

MEDICAL MUTINY

"The duty of a true health professional of any kind is to protect its patients from its government, from its medical boards and anyone who restricts their ability to practise medicine and provide true informed consent."
Dr Bryan Ardis – Otto, Brave Series, Episode 1, 2022

THE WORLD DOCTORS' ALLIANCE

Established on 15 January, 2020 The World Doctors' Alliance is an independent non-profit alliance of doctors, nurses, healthcare professionals and staff around the world who united in the wake of the Covid-19 response chapter to share experiences with a view to ending all lockdowns and related damaging measures and to re-establish universal health determinance of psychological and physical wellbeing for all humanity.

Take off your masks and welcome to our side for freedom.

Molecular biologist and immunologist Professor Dolories Cahill announced to the world on behalf of the Alliance that the coronavirus is a seasonal virus and for people who have symptoms, there are effective treatments. There is no need for masks, lockdown, for fear, social distancing or for putting people into quarantine.

Professor Cahill spoke about a new food movement, a new health movement and the need to brand restaurants, airlines and businesses that respect our right for freedom and freedom of speech.

Vice President, Dr Heiko Schoning declared: "We see no evidence of a medical pandemic so it looks like a 'plandemic' and we don't want this new normal and we don't want to go back to the old normal because the old normal created this situation of new normal. We want a better normal and we want it together, with you (Latter-Day Media, 2020)."

Dr Heiko Schoning from Hamburg, Germany became known when arrested by the Jackboots for speaking at the World Freedom Rally in Berlin in 2020 with Robert F Kennedy Jr. He was instrumental in founding the ACU, the Corona Extra-Parliamentary Inquiry Committee, to delve into the Corona story and says, "If parliament does not do it, we, the citizens, are called upon to do it ourselves." The ACU began on 3 July, 2020 and is widening its investigations to evolve into an international enquiry. In 2019, Dr Schoning warned the people of the coming 'plandemic' and he names perpetrators in his book, *Game Over: COVID-19 – ANTHRAX-01*.

THE OLD MAN IN THE CHAIR

Dr Vernon Coleman MB, ChB, DSc, FRSA, a member of The World Doctors' Alliance, also known as 'The Old Man in The Chair', as he is known in his podcasts called out the 'plandemic' from the very beginning. He has been banned from mainstream media, vilified on the internet and admits that 'telling the truth is not always fun'. He has been a guiding light, offering information and support to the people through videos and articles throughout the unfolding Covid story. For decades, Dr Coleman has been warning of the scenario we now find ourselves in through his numerous books. His voice resonates with reason and wisdom.

He said, "Now is the time for the medical and nursing professions to stand up and to demand some answers and explanations from the leaders of their professions and from the administrators who gave the orders which have led to tens of thousands of unnecessary deaths."

And: "If we allow these sad and sorry creatures to defeat us it will be like the Brazilian football team being thrashed by a team of one-legged pirates with the scurvy (Coleman, 2022)."

FREEDOM AIRWAYS

The World Doctor's Alliance President, Professor Dolores Cahill, is co-founder of Freedom Airways and one of a small group of people creating an airline that respects freedom and human rights. No masks, no social distancing, no jabs, no contact tracing. The goal originally was to fly between countries that are open and steer the tourist sector to boost the economy of those countries. I was saddened to hear Professor Cahill say that the most interest in the project came from Australians wishing to leave the country.

Activist, musician, author of videos, radio shows and documentaries, Max Igan who has for years been alerting us to the totalitarian tiptoe we are now seeing galloping at a tremendous speed, fled the country in fear for his safety and wellbeing. His bank accounts were frozen by the Australian Jackboots. Despite having to leave everything behind, he has now resettled and is continuing to support the people and to keep them informed through his website The CrowHouse.

In the year 2000, I met a psychologist who was a student in the course I was attending. He confided that he was updating his qualifications and then would be taking his family to live in another country. Australia, he said, was heading in a precarious direction, and he had seen it all before. There also was an aspect of being afraid for his safety as he had been vocal about the electorate system that he believed to be corrupted. The manipulation of electoral results has been under scrutiny for a long time as an avenue the Giant could be using to place its 'merrymen' into positions of power.

In May 2022, Australia went to the polls and it was evident that people were waking up to the fact that governance for the people, by the people, had long ago been usurped, if it ever existed. An unprecedented number of people refused to vote and take part in an unlawful system. Many chose to put the two major opposing parties last on the voting paper, electing to vote for the few candidates who were fighting for the people's rights. A two-party system had long ago been set up in Australian politics – same bird with two wings or same doll, different dress, Dr Christiane Northrup would say.

This is not my story to tell.

However, when walking away from the voting booths on that day in May 2022, the voice of a volunteer handing out leaflets could be heard, enticing people to vote for the candidate she represented. "I want my job back," she said. I heard the pain and I felt the desperation behind those words.

Mum, in her later years confided that she gave the 'Pooh' vote – meaning that she wrote the word, 'pooh' on the ballot paper and gleefully placed it in the appropriate box. And, I believe, she did.

Perhaps we have seen the last of what many have described as the election 'clown show'. If not, then next time, the 'pooh vote' it is!

Australian Health Professionals Speak Out

COVID MEDICAL NETWORK
Primum Non Nocere – First, Do No Harm

The Covid Medical Network (CMN) was founded in 2020 by a group of senior medical doctors and health professionals who were concerned about the health impacts of the lockdowns used in response to the SARS-coV-2 outbreaks in Victoria and across Australia. They were also concerned about the lack of good information available to the general public and the misleading use of data. They said, "These factors have created an unwarranted state of fear in people."

On 12 February, 2021 the Covid Medical Network was issued with a Cease and Desist letter by the Therapeutic Goods Administration (TGA) to take down the 'Early Treatments' section from their website. If an adequate and approved treatment for SARS-coV-2 had been available at the time, then injections could not have been mandated. Could this have been a factor in banning and vilifying treatments that many health professionals were claiming to be safe and effective? The Jackboots were quick to respond to these claims by arresting doctors, taking away their medical credentials, raiding pharmacies and increasing media manipulation. Science that did not support the narrative was labelled, 'misinformation' and the scientists involved could be persecuted under the new laws that make it illegal to spread 'misinformation'.

On 11 August, 2021 the Covid Medical Network addressed a letter to doctors, health professionals and fellow Australians detailing their concerns regarding the government's response to the 'pandemic'. In this they wrote, "We believe there is a better way forward for Victorians and all Australians. A path founded on the principles of good medical practice, including, openness and honesty, humility and consultation, collaboration and respect for autonomy, to always encourage with Care, Hope and Reassurance, never to provoke Fear Panic or Terror."

The Covid Medical Network addressed an Open Letter, dated 8 March, 2022 to Professor Crawford, Dr Murphy, Professor Kelly, Professor Skerritt, the Hon Minister Hunt, members of Australian Technical Advisory Group on Immunisation (ATAGI), the Therapeutic Goods Association (TGA) and the Federal Health Department. Documentation to show that the vaccines are not 'safe and effective' was presented and it was requested that any information saying they are 'safe' be withdrawn. It also requested that these vaccines be withdrawn from public availability and a halt to the rollout to children, happen as a matter of urgency.

Pauline Hanson's One Nation Party called for a Royal Commission into the Covid management by the Australian governments and cited this letter as another reason why this must happen. The Open Letter can be viewed at the One Nation website.

The Covid Medical Network is now the Australian Medical Network.

However, it was becoming apparent that only the government narrative was permitted and all other information was considered to be misinformation. Australian doctors were being subjected to harsh reprisals such as losing their licence to practise medicine, gaol time, fines and a visit from the Australian Jackboots due to the new 'draconian rules'. An excerpt from AHPRA'S statement sent to doctors on 9 March, 2021 said, 'There is no place for an anti-vaccination message in professional practice'.

Medical professionals from around the world were reporting retaliation from the medical establishment for non-compliance. United States attorney, Aaron Siri, told of the snowballing effect when Dr Patricia Lee courageously stepped forward after being ignored by public health officials when she tried to report the jab injuries she was seeing. He said that doctors then contacted his office and eleven had signed declarations to attest to the injuries they had witnessed. He went on to say that physicians are afraid, even though some are injured from the jab and many have lost their licence to practise.

However, a few brave practitioners risked the Jackboots' wrath to uphold their personal integrity. I once heard a paediatrician say that the bowl of fruit in his surgery had received more childhood vaccinations than the arms of young children visiting his practice. Today the 'bowl of fruit' is sitting in a few surgeries but the Jackboots' intent to silence and punish those in opposition to the official narrative was becoming an increased threat.

In 2021 an independent Canadian journalist, Anthony Murdoch, reported on how Pastor Artur Pawlowski kept his church open during the peak of the Covid-19 story, ordering the Canadian Jackboots to leave the church when they interrupted with Gestapo-like tactics. He and his brother were arrested after giving a church service. They were stopped on the highway, surrounded by multiple police cars, dragged onto the road and handcuffed. Both were charged with 'organising an illegal in-person gathering', but these charges were later successfully overturned by the Court of Appeal of Alberta.

Pastor Pawlowski was later to reveal the treatment he was subjected to when imprisoned for fifty-one days, saying he was placed in a metal box, stripped naked, searched and spent many hours on concrete. It was chilling to hear him say that prison guards coerced inmates to 'beat him up', however, heartening to hear that they refused. He spent time in a 'mental health unit' and at the time of writing, is under strict 'house arrest' while facing ten years in prison (Murdoch, 2022).

Pastor Pawlowski was a champion for the Canadian Truckers. "Stand up for your rights," he told them when arrested for attempting to carry out a service at their request.

Dr Simone Gold, a board certified emergency doctor, an attorney and founder of America's Frontline Doctors, was arrested in January 2022 and sentenced to prison for sixty days on a false misdemeanour trespassing charge. This esteemed doctor was subjected to a violent assault from an FBI SWAT team (in full war regalia) battering down her door and stampeding into her home to handcuff the doctor who spoke truth the government did not want the people to hear.

DR MARK HOBART

Dr Mark Hobart, a director of the Covid Medical Network was one doctor who was vocal about the Covid data manipulation and fraud on a global scale. He paid a heavy price when his Australian Sunshine North Clinic was shut down because he refused to release private patient records. Morgan C Jonas, who was present at the scene, recorded the incident when seven authorised Jackboots from the Department of Health seized confidential patient files, the appointment book and various other documents. Dr Hobart was told that under the new laws, there is no such thing as patient confidentiality.

Author and independent investigative journalist Mark Taliano said, "Dr Mark Hobart is the ONLY doctor who cared for the elderly in his community in 2020 when other doctors abandoned them. He's the ONLY doctor who spoke up against locking up the elderly alone in their room for four months. Dr Mark Hobart is also the ONLY doctor who wrote to Brett Sutton about testing the elderly prior to jabbing them."

In 2022, when being interviewed by investigative journalist Maria Zeee, Dr Hobart called on paediatricians and obstetricians to speak out on behalf of their patients to stop this dangerous vaccine and to protect the children. He said that it is heart-retching for him to see innocent children being sacrificed to this vaccine.

Maria Zeee offered a platform from which to speak for any practitioner taking up the challenge.

DOCTORS SPEAKING UP IS A MATTER OF HONOUR

In May 2022, Australian journalist, Maria Zeee interviewed Australian doctors in a Conference of Conscience series. She explained that these warriors had finally decided to speak about the ways the government and the TGA (Therapeutic Goods Administration) skewed the safety and efficacy data of the Covid-19 jabs and the danger of continuing the vaccination program.

Maria Zeee said Australians are beginning to show courage and that is because alternative media platforms are giving them a place to speak. It is indeed. She said the Australian public have been waiting a very long time for the doctors to come out and speak publicly.

Dr Christopher Neil specialising in cardiology and President of Australian Medical Professional Society (AMPS) said, "It is time for all of us to put away our passivity and any lack of courage – this is now a matter of honour – we know that what the Australian people have been subjected to is not right and not good. Doctors speaking up is a matter of honour."

Dr John Piesse had faced the wrath of the Jackboots when assisting parents to receive exemptions from mandatory vaccines for early-age children. He reported on the International Agreement made in 2019 called the Trusted News Initiative and said that all major organisations had agreed to not publish anything that was not consistent with the vaccine promoted narrative. The once respected newspapers such as *The Australian* and *The Age* will not say a word about the dangers and harm caused by the jabs. He said that people are being indoctrinated and unreceptive to anything that is not in the mainstream media.

Dr Joseph Goldbaum said, "When you suppress freedom of speech you are also suppressing freedom of thought."

The Universal Declaration of Human Rights (1948) says: "Everyone has the right to freedom of opinion and expression. This right includes freedom to hold opinions without interference and to seek, receive and impart information and ideas through any media."

Geriatrician, Dr Shoba Iyer said she could not ignore her conscience any longer and called to her colleagues to break their silence on the effects from the Covid jabs she believed they must be seeing. She revealed that she has pages of doctor documented injuries and that these are not mild, such as recurring cancer, rapid dementia decline, autoimmune conditions, strokes, heart attacks and the list is long.

Doctors were afraid of the consequences if they talked about what they were witnessing and those who did, were shut down. However, Dr Iyer said, "This is what we do as doctors, protect our patients."

Dr William Bay founded a movement called the Queensland People's Protest to bring awareness to the gradual loss of medical freedoms in the state. He called for his colleagues to join with the people of Australia and stop enforcing dangerous vaccines and to stand with him to ensure that an ethical medical system is not lost forever. He wore a stethoscope around his neck and blew the battle-horn before beginning a quest, one being to 'crash' a three-day Australian Medical Association (AMA) conference held in Sydney with guests such as Dr Anthony Fauci, Professor Brendan Murphy, Dr Vijay Roach, Dr Anne Tonkin and Dr Raina MacIntyre. He informed those present that they were on notice from the people of Queensland through the Queensland People's Protest (Debtstop, 2022).

Dr Bay walked the streets of Brisbane calling for people to become aware of his concerns regarding the Covid jab. He took the Road Less Travelled and was suspended by AHPRA in August, 2022 for speaking out against the Government narrative.

On 10 September, 2022 Dr Phillip Altman spoke at the Australian Medical Professional Society (AMPS). His speech drew a line in the sand. No longer could any health professional, health regulatory body or Member of Parliament not be aware of the Covid evidence-based data regarding vaccine injuries and death. This is because a letter was sent summarising this information together with Dr Altman's report titled, *A Time of Covid*.

This information can be seen at Australian Medical Professionals Society (AMPS).

Dr Altman's talk was brutal and factual regarding many aspects of the Covid story. He said that plans were being put into place to build facilities to produce more gene-based therapies and believed that we would probably be forced to be injected with these failed technologies every year in future. He said: "The nightmare is likely to repeat itself unless we do something and we must." And, "Australia was chosen as a testing ground for some of the worst ruthless and brutal lockdown and mandatory vaccines ever seen, it must be Australia that leads the way back."

Tears dripped from Dr Altman's voice when he thanked the Freedom Fighters for holding the line, those that protest and express opposition to the Giant's agenda, those in the fight for the future of humanity (The Editor, *Cairns News, 2022*).

Dr Altman has a Bachelor of Pharmacy (Hons), a Bachelor and Masters of Science and a Doctor of Philosophy. He worked as a clinical trial and regulatory affairs pharmaceutical industry consultant with more than forty years of experience in designing, managing and reporting clinical trials.

NURSES SPEAK OUT

Nurses worldwide began to speak about the unethical Covid rules and the denigrating consequences to the ethical standards in nursing care.

Mary Jane Stevens, an emergency nurse working in Brisbane, Australia, courageously spoke at Senator Malcolm Roberts' The COVID Enquiry 2.0 held on 17 August, 2022. She described her experiences when witnessing the devastating injuries that occurred post vaccine, about the coercive measures in the hospital to vaccinate the staff and her own adverse reactions when receiving the jab. When asked for her opinion on the situation regarding Queensland Health, she replied that it was in a state of collapse. Ms Stevens said that she was representing nurses who were sacked because they did not want to be part of an experiment. As a consequence, thousands of fit and healthy nurses are not able to work and an understaffed situation is creating chaos.

The Editor, *Cairns News* (2022) reported on a meeting held on the Gold Coast, Australia, where whistleblower nurse, Debbie Jane Harris spoke about vaccine adverse events including stillbirths, deformed babies, blood clots and cancer remissions reversed. She said that only six Covid-positive cases had been seen in ICU in twenty months, all had been discharged and some were double vaccinated. While health officials, politicians and the media were claiming hospitals were being overloaded with Covid cases, she told how the special Covid ward had been locked up and left empty for months and months and months.

A recently retired doctor spoke on the censorship of doctors by the Australian Health Practitioners Regulatory Agency (AHPRA). This included deregistration of doctors who speak out against the vaccine rollout policy. Ms Harris said nurses had received the same directive and were also told their social media would be monitored. They had been encouraged to 'dob' on any colleagues involved in spreading anti-vaccine information.

This is soul wounding.

WHY AUSTRALIA REMAINS A PENAL COLONY FOR PHYSICIANS

Doctors who dare to discuss COVID medical matters lose their incomes.

This letter was published by the *Orthomolecular Medicine News Service* on 27 July, 2022 and edited by Dr Andrew W Saul. He wrote the following. When licensed, experienced medical doctors are silenced and even actively persecuted for discussing a public health issue, something is very wrong. Here is a report recently received from an Australian physician, fully qualified and with 40 years' experience. The doctor has been expelled from the medical profession because of questioning the prevailing Covid narrative.

"I was suspended by the medical board of Australia on May the 28th, 2020 by the AHPRA committee (medical board of Australia). This was because I had writings on Facebook pages that included criticisms of the medical system, the side effects of drugs and the problems caused to patients by hospital treatment.

"Even though I did not use my name as a medical GP on these Facebook pages, the medical board still identified me as the doctor speaking out and therefore considered this a crime. Because of this,

I was referred to VCAT, a sort of kangaroo court in Melbourne, which confirmed this to be a grievous criminal act, and under a specific section of the law I was considered to be such a risk that my suspension was agreed upon.

"In my 40 years of general practice, I have never harmed a patient.

"I have always had an interest in integrative medicine. I had been suggesting to my patients that they support their immune systems with vitamin C, vitamin D, magnesium and zinc. I was always concerned to look at the basic cause behind an illness. The merry-go-round in general practice has been so monetised that you are only a good doctor if you see six patients an hour. In the past 10 years medical practice has deteriorated to an extent that conventional medical practice is now completely allopathic, and in the hands of Big Pharma.

"I was suspended because I criticised Big Pharma and also was concerned about the amount of persecution doctors already had from AHPRA. I noticed that some doctors who had been suspended and criminalised by this organisation had committed suicide.

"After a conference between the medical defence attorneys and AHPRA in a few months' time, I will then have to face the final countdown in May 2023. I expect they're going to use every kind of ammunition to criminalise me and show I put out critical information on Facebook pages, which they think is anathema to public safety.

"This is happening to a lot of doctors around the world.

"My problem is that now I have no way to support myself financially. I currently exist on a bank loan and this was given to me before I had realized that I was going to be suspended for such a length of time, that I would not be able to recuperate my losses through alternative work.

"The Medical Board of Australia has laws requiring that any doctor who is suspended is not allowed to work in the health system or in integrative health in any way whatsoever. I am precluded from working in the health field which I know so much about because I have excellent qualifications in medicine and in integrative health.

"Doctors in Australia are unable to speak out about integrative health, social determinants of health, vitamin therapy, or anything that does not deal with drugs. If I criticise psychiatry, and talk about the serious side effects caused by psychoactive drugs, or discuss chemotherapy and the side effects thereof, this is unacceptable.

"I am concerned about the way people are often overlooked and mistreated in hospitals. My personal experience with my in-laws has confirmed that patients are often treated as if they are diseases and not people.

"I now realise that we are all in the midst of a straight-jacketing of the whole community. Australia has become in essence a police state. So many people have lost their jobs and mental illness has skyrocketed because of the fear engendered by the media's coverage of Covid. I feel so sympathetic to all these people whose lives are being ruined by the shutdowns and isolation caused by the way governments have dealt with the pandemic."

Dr Andrew Saul said that this problem is by no means limited to Australia. Having read the doctor's letter, it will be appreciated why he published it anonymously. He had seen similar reports from Singapore, UK, Finland, USA, China and several other countries.

Dr Andrew Saul passed away on 3 February, 2024. A true warrior of the Spirit, his decades of work in orthomolecular and nutritional medicine will be ongoing to assist others through this time of transition. He will be sadly missed.

Sayer Ji said in a tribute, "Dr Saul often noted that 'We need more healers instead of salesmen'. May we rise to fill this void by embracing his shining example. With gratitude, Dr Saul – your service and wisdom are forever medicine."

NZDSOS

New Zealand Doctors Speaking Out With Science

NZDSOS is made up of Doctors, Dentists, Pharmacists and Vets and has formed an alliance with other groups locally and internationally

NZDSOS was established in 2021 and created an online clinic to assist those affected by Covid-19 symptoms and to collect and collate data on the adverse effects of the Covid vaccines. They help those in need by supplying food and seed as well as those involved in legal actions.

Locally, the Wakaminenga Health Council (WHC) was established to promote a new understanding between health professionals and the people of New Zealand: Taurite (Balance) through Reretahi (Harmony), Kotahitanga (Unity) and Tapu (Holism), leading to Hauora – Manaakitanga (Health –Wellbeing).

Internationally, the NZDSOS is a founding member of the World Council for Health that has been formed as an alternative to the WHO and stands to be free of governmental and corporate influence.

NZDSOS state on their website: "We have written many letters to all government and regulatory bodies pointing out scientific findings regarding Covid-19, the Pfizer injection and early treatment and, as well as providing details of death and injury caused by the injection. The replies we have received completely ignored our concerns and statements."

Psychiatrist, Dr Emanuel Garcia was a founding member of NZDSOS and he said, "There are nearly thirty thousand doctors in the Medical Council's register. Of those thirty thousand a pittance has joined with New Zealand Doctors Speaking Out With Science to stand up for these foundational principles of our profession. I am certain that if a mere ten percent of practising physicians in New Zealand publicly affirmed the basic principles of medicine, we would not be living through the hell of the tyranny imposed by the government in the name of what they call 'medicine' but which every physician understands is merely an Orwellian caricature."

THE PATH OF COURAGE

SEE YOU AT THE BARRICADES

"Even the smallest person can change the future."
J R R Tolkien

It appeared that the legal community were slow to act, however, there were those who had been fighting for years and some for decades. Dr Reiner Fuellmich reported that the number stepping up to support the people was growing every day. However, it was also becoming apparent that the Giant and its 'merrymen' had infiltrated and corrupted a profession that had sworn to uphold a sacred duty.

The following lawyers had either been in the 'fight' for a long time or were among the first to support the rights of the people when the Covid narrative was introduced.

PETER FAM

Peter Fam is the principal lawyer at Maat's Method. He founded the firm to support those who had been censored for speaking against the Giant's narrative and to uphold human rights and universal law.

It is the only non-government human rights law firm in Australia. He is a director of Children's Health Defense, Australian Chapter.

From the beginning of the Covid story, Peter Fam worked on the issues surrounding the narrative such as privacy, informed consent and employment law involving vaccine mandates.

Peter Fam was interviewed by Kara Thomas, Secretary of AMPS (Australian Medical Professional Society) on Discussions from the Frontline. He said that when receiving the backlash from writing articles questioning the validity of the public health orders, "I had a choice to make like many Australians and the choice was, do I remain authentic, do I follow my principles, do what I believe to be true and just or, do I improvise?"

He said that the only way he could remain true to himself was to start his own firm.

"Maat is the Kemetic (Ancient Egyptian) deity of Truth, Justice and Balance."

DR REINER FUELLMICH

Dr Reiner Fuellmich, a lawyer licenced in Germany and California (USA), successfully convicted Volkswagen for the modified catalytic converters issue and the Deutsche Bank, he defined as being a criminal enterprise.

On 10 July, 2020 Dr Fuellmich co-founded the Berlin Corona Investigative Committee (Corona Ausschuss). The Committee interviewed medical professionals, scientists, lawyers and many other experts to gain factual insight into the coronavirus events and the consequences. These interviews were recorded and broadcast for the world to view.

This led to the Grand Jury the Court of Public Opinion that began on 5 February, 2022. An international team of medical professionals, members from the scientific community, economists and others came together to see what could be proven to-date.

Dr Fuellmich said, "These are the facts that will pull the masks off the faces of all those responsible for these crimes. To the politicians who believe those corrupt people, these facts are hereby offered as a lifeline that can help you readjust your course of action, and start the long overdue public scientific discussion, and not go down with those charlatans and criminals."

In October, 2022 Dr Fuellmich announced that his next venture was to broaden the scope of the investigation through the International Crimes Investigative Committee (ICIC.LAW), he founded.

Dr Fuellmich said: "These are the worst crimes against humanity ever committed."

JULIAN GILLESPIE

The following excerpt is from an interview Julian Gillespie gave on 23 March, 2022 to Covid Under Question, hosted by Senator Malcolm Roberts.

Julian Gillespie, a former Australian lawyer and barrister came out of retirement to support the people to stop the Covid-19 jab based on the number of deaths already recorded. He is a director of Children's Health Defence, Australian Chapter.

Julian Gillespie told Covid Under Question that these 'vaccines' have not undergone geno-toxicity or carcinogenic trials. He reported that no mRNA technology has successfully made it to market and this and other critical and enlightening medical information had been placed before the Secretary. Further, evidence was given to the FDA on 25 September, 2020 that the Pfizer clinical trials were affected by fraud. He talked about the known variances in batches with some people receiving lethal doses.

Julian Gillespie said that the jackboot had been placed on informed consent, snuffing out legal right in this country and indeed on the sanctity of the patient/doctor relationship. If a medical doctor with years of experience questioned the efficacy or safety of these procedures, they were immediately to be referred to as an anti-vaxxer or an individual providing misinformation.

ROBERT F KENNEDY JR

Lawyer, author, activist, son of Robert F Kennedy and nephew of John F Kennedy.

At the beginning of the Covid-19 story, Robert F Kennedy Jr told the people, "See you at the barricades".

However, he has for decades been fighting in the courts to cease the poisoning of our planet. He has taken on giants such as Du Pont and Monsanto to bring to light the glyphosate issue, and winning. He fought battles on issues such as acid rain, ozone, coal ash, PCB's, hydrocarbons and numerous other poisons. He fought the pharmaceutical giants to cease harming the children and pregnant women through vaccines and pharmaceuticals containing neurotoxic mercury. He wrote the books, spoke at the rallies and brought together his understanding of law, human rights, science and the global predators to get the information out into the world. He is chief legal counsel for Children's Health Defense, an online platform offering information and support.

Robert F Kennedy Jr commented that his family have been in a literal fist fight with the CIA for a long time and he would never ask anyone to speak out as he has done, others do not have the support and resources to survive the backlash. However, he said that now is the time to ask just that – we all must take a stand and fight.

David Icke's (2010) research revealed that John F Kennedy had signed an Executive Order allowing the US Treasury Secretary to issue $4.29 billion in interest-free money, bypassing the Rothschild privately owned banking system, the Federal Reserve. In the same year, Kennedy was assassinated. His successor, Lyndon Johnson, rescinded the policy. Kennedy also opposed the Israeli nuclear programme and the Vietnam War. His brother, Robert Kennedy was later assassinated. Icke says that the Rothschilds and the Kennedys have been at war ever since.

THE JACKBOOTS

When speaking of John F Kennedy, the former Governor of Minnesota, Jesse Ventura (2010) wrote: "What I respect most about the man is that he was willing to grow and change his views while in office, for the sake of the greater good. Without his going up against the generals who wanted to attack Cuba and take out the Soviet missiles in the fall of 1962, I wouldn't be sitting here today writing this book. We'd have all been victims of a nuclear holocaust."

He said, "Robert F Kennedy was only 42 when he was assassinated and, having just won the California primary, he was on his way to the Democratic nomination and likely the presidency. He would have begun withdrawing our troops from Vietnam and saved thousands of American lives. He'd already been talking with his aides about reopening the investigation into who killed his brother. I think it's safe to say that, if he'd lived, we'd have a different kind of country than what we've become. Robert would have led a compassionate revolution – because he was a man not only of courage, but of compassion."

When interviewed by Dr Patrick Gentempo in 2021, Robert F Kennedy Jr said, "In my lifetime, there have been three pandemics where zero-liability vaccines were rushed to the market, and then had to be withdrawn because of injuries." He said they did it with AZT in the 1980's and then the swine flu shot. "Both of those were phoney pandemics, and forced millions of people around the world to take very, very dangerous, untested zero-liability vaccines that ultimately had to be withdrawn."

According to many, we are here again, but this time, it is on a world scale.

Robert F Kennedy Jr's book, *The Real Anthony Fauci: Big Pharma's Global War on Democracy, Humanity and Public Health*, gives insight into the story.

The swine flu pandemic was exposed to be a mild flu but not before the roll out of vaccines that caused death and disability.

Eleanor McBean PhD, ND wrote in her book, *Swine Flu Expose*, 'There is no swine flu epidemic in the US or anywhere in the world, and there is not going to be one either unless the vaccine promoters carry out their plans to vaccinate all people; then there will be a full blown epidemic of vaccine poisoning – not flu.'

When interviewed by Gary Null PhD (1996), biochemist, Kary Mullis, the discoverer of PCR technology, said that he could not find any scientific evidence to say HIV causes AIDS. He stressed that people are taking a very dangerous drug called AZT that can cause death if taken in sufficient amounts. He said, "Aids is the pendulum swinging back to the right – less permissiveness – people that don't pay attention to their grandmother's code of ethics suffer for it."

The Perth Group, originally led by biophysicist Eleni Papadopulos-Eleopulos, emergency physician Val Turner and Professor John Papadimitriou formed in 1981 at the Royal Perth Hospital. They argued with science that the HIV retrovirus has not been shown to exist. They say that pharmacological data proves AZT is toxic to all cells and may cause cases of AIDS.

Today, the same storyline has enabled toxic drugs to be approved when safe and effective treatments are available.

TONY NIKOLIC

Tony Nikolic, lawyer and criminologist fighting for the people's freedom is the General Manager of AFL Solicitors in Australia. He is an Australian Medical Network board member and a lawyer in The Grand Jury the Court of Public Opinion.

When speaking with Dr Reiner Fuellmich in August 2021, he said the people of Australia were waking up and standing for human rights. People from all walks of life were expressing concern and support.

Tony Nikolic talked about media manipulation, pointing out the Prime Minister facing the media and saying there is a choice and the next day calling for mandates for workers in hospitals, aged-care workers and students. He said that deaths and admissions to hospital were going up in correlation with the jab rollout.

AFL Solicitors legally support doctors who are threatened with deregistration on a daily basis, those fighting the mandates and others who have received unjust Covid fines.

Tony Nikolic said: "You are born free, free to choose, freedom from arbitrary detention, freedom of bodily integrity. Don't give it away for free."

SERENE TEFFAHA

Serene Teffaha, an Australian lawyer, was one of the first to launch class actions against the unlawful pandemic response measures.

She told Jonathan Otto (Vaccine Secrets: Reloaded, 2021): *"They took my licence, but not my voice."*

"The worst happened, now they have made you unstoppable," Jonathan Otto suggested.

"We are all going to be attacked. We need to move into, 'What about our future, what about our children?' Natural laws will unfold and if something is not working right, then it will change."

Serene Teffaha founded *AdvocateMe* to assist people to deal with government conflict such as Cops for Covid Truth and Teachers for Covid Truth. She said that governance has been usurped by private global interests, corruption has reached a peak and even judges have been usurped.

AdvocateMe is a safe platform for people to share their stories, have access to templates and find information. For example: science showing that the mask is wrong. In 1918 bacteria killed people because of the vaccines and wearing the mask was a double whammy – the mask alone killed and now masks are weaponised.

Serene Teffaha said: "Anti-vaxxers are some of the most educated people in our community. Those who are being attacked are the thinkers. This is where democracy fails because it says the majority wins but, what if the majority are stupid?"

And, "Our freedoms are not taken away, we give them away. Connecting with each other is important now. Stop being a 'know it all'– stop judging, be humble and listen more. We are going up against a really big bully system. Perhaps even think of building alternative communities and creating a new story. The battle lines have been drawn."

THE GRAND JURY THE COURT OF PUBLIC OPINION

INJUSTICE TO ONE IS AN INJUSTICE TO ALL

In February 2022, the findings of the Berlin Corona Investigative Committee were officially presented to the Grand Jury the Court of Public Opinion.

The Grand Jury the Court of Public Opinion, 'of the people, for the people and by the people' was held to reveal the crimes inflicted upon the world by governments and organisations under the guise of protecting it against a Covid pandemic. Based on natural law, it was independently heard from the present system of courts of law, government or any non-government organisation and supported by the Berlin Corona Investigative Committee.

Dr Reiner Fuellmich said in his opening address: "There is no corona pandemic but only a PCR test 'plandemic' fuelled by an elaborate psychological operation designed to create a constant state of panic among the world's population. This agenda has been long planned, is ultimately unsuccessful and is a follow on from the swine flu pandemic some years ago.

"It was cooked up by a group of super rich psychopathic and sociopathic people who hate and fear people at the same time. They have no empathy and are driven by the desire to obtain full control over all of us, the people of the world. They are using our governments and the media, both which they literally own, to convey their panic propaganda twenty-four seven."

Dr Fuellmich explained that our governments have been taken over through avenues such as the World Economic Forum's Young Global Leaders' program. This was originally called, 'Global Leaders for Tomorrow'. It began in 1993 and in 2004 became 'Young Global Leaders'. Graduates from this programme that you will recognise are: billionaire eugenicist Bill Gates, German Chancellor Angela Merkel, Canadian Prime Minister Justin Trudeau, New Zealand's Prime Minister Jacinda Ardern, Australian Health Minister Greg Hunt and former British Prime Minister Tony Blair.

For many years I have listened to doctors and scientists speak about the poisoning of our food, air and water, the effects of pharmaceutical medications and especially the vaccinations on the population and the children. However, nothing prepared me for the heartache experienced when listening to the brilliant men and women who testified. When hearing the tears in their voices when speaking of the crimes being committed against humanity, especially, the children.

On day four, Professor Dr Eucharist Bhakdi (microbiologist, immunologist and infection biologist - Germany), acknowledged that a first-year medical student would know the dangers of the Covid experimental jab that is being mandated on a whole world. He stated that no-one should be allowed to practise medicine if they profess to not know.

Dr Bhakdi said: "People are killing our children and it looks premeditated. How can we stand to see this happen? There is only one conversation to have, the death and injury so far seen is testimony to stop these 'vaccines' immediately as set out in the Nuremberg Codex."

When speaking against the government Covid-19 narrative, this esteemed doctor was charged in connection with two statements he made in April and September, 2021 and will be facing a hearing at the Lower Court, Plon, Germany.

Although some health care providers spoke up, others remained silent and abandoned ethical duty, bodily autonomy and informed consent.

During the Nuremberg Trials, nurses accused of participation in the experimentation carried out on prisoners were not exempt from prosecution when offering the excuses of following orders, keeping jobs and feeding families.

In today's world, health care workers in hospitals and nursing homes are witness to the deaths from following a government mandated procedure that involved the use of ventilators and treating with drugs such as midazolam or remdesivir. Dr Bryan Ardis, a chiropractor, acupuncturist and medical researcher, brought the world's attention to these protocols that were part of a pathway that was being redirected from healing to one leading to the death of many people.

Remdesivir, a drug known to cause heart, liver and kidney failure was the drug of choice. On 1 May, 2020 the US Food and Drug Administration (FDA) approved the Emergency Use Authorisation (EUA) for remdesivir to be used to treat hospitalised patients diagnosed with Covid-19. By 2022, in the United States of America, it was the authorised drug treatment for paediatric groups and the only authorised drug for 'Covid treatment' to be used in hospitals, in nursing homes and infusion centres.

In the United Kingdom, a protocol using morphine and midazolam called, 'End of Life Care' was introduced into nursing homes.

Deaths resulting from these protocols were recorded as being from Covid-19.

Dr Bryan Ardis' testimony on day three, titled *PCR-Test*, tells the story.

Dr Mike Yeadon in an interview on Radical with Maajid Nawaz (2022) discussed the dangers of midazolam and morphine combined. He said that midazolam, like other CNS depressants (opioids, barbiturates) may produce respiratory depression. This is especially likely to occur in patients who are receiving other CNS depressants concurrently and in patients with pre-existing disease.

Dr Yeadon, former Vice-President and Chief Scientist of Allergy and Respiratory Research for Pfizer, told Maajid Nawaz, "There is no evidence whatsoever of a new virus causing massive illness and death." He explained that there were no excess deaths until the government introduced the new measures – lockdown, masking, social distancing, business closures, border restrictions, mass testing and an assumption that people without symptoms could be sources of infection.

Dr Yeadon said that the public health departments of every country imposing these restrictions knew for a fact before they were used that they did not work because scientists at the World Health Organisation (WHO) conducted a meta-analysis in 2019 that found every measure not to be useful. He said that the chronic fear-driven and immune-suppressant narrative was amplified by the media, twenty-four seven. Excess deaths in care homes can be explained by government protocols introduced through the health systems for the purpose of ending lives.

Dr Pierre Kory, (founding member of FLCCC (Frontline Covid-19 Critical Care Alliance) and Pulmonary and Critical Care Specialist) when addressing United States Senator Ron Johnson's, 'A Second Opinion on Covid' said, "Hospitals have become dangerous places for sick people. Patients must do whatever they can to avoid the hospital as when imprisoned in a hospital they are denied their rights.

"They are not allowed a patient advocate and their families are denied access to patients. They are prisoners in the system. They have no rights and get the treatment dictated by the hospital. They are dangerous places for sick people."

Many who would have treated themselves at home with successful protocols used for influenza, went to the hospital in fear that they had contracted a 'deadly' virus and may have been subjected to these protocols.

The Truth for Health Team reported on 7 September, 2022 that attorneys, Dan Watkins and Michael Hamilton had announced in a National Press Conference that they had filed the first lawsuits against hospitals and doctors in Fresno, California. This action was taken on behalf of grieving families who lost loved ones to the 'bounties' paid to hospitals for using the toxic combination of food and fluid restriction, remdesivir, mechanical ventilation and the high dose morphine-midazolam combination protocol.

Have you ever wondered what you would have done if living during a previous reign of terror? Well now you know! Many are still sleeping from the potent elixir ingested from the Giant's distillery. Some are 'sitting on the fence' waiting to 'get back to normal'. Humpty dumpty sat on the fence – how did that end, I ask you?

Eddie Jaku (2020), a survivor of two German concentration camps, said in his memoir, "It was madness, in the true sense of the word - otherwise civilised people lost all ability to tell right from wrong. They committed terrible atrocities, and worse, they enjoyed it." He tells us, "If enough people had stood up then, *Kristallnacht* and said, 'Enough! What are you doing? What is wrong with you? Then the course of history would have been different. But, they did not. They were scared. They were weak. And their weaknesses allowed them to be manipulated into hatred."

We The People are indebted to the Attorneys at Law, Judge Rui Fonseca E Castro (Portugal) and the expert witnesses for shining light on the background and the planning behind the Giant's attempt to harness the human body and mind. And, I believe, an attempt to disconnect humanity from soul and spirit. With this foundation, it is now possible to move toward bringing those responsible, and those who have carried out this agenda, to face justice.

THE GRAND JURY THE COURT OF PUBLIC OPINION – A CONCLUSION

Resource: David Sorensen (founder of the website, *StopWorldControl*, holds a master's degree in media and communication from the University of Science and Arts in Ghent, Belgium).

From the many testimonies heard, it became apparent that what we are witnessing is an attempt by private entities to take over the world by using governmental authorities and health agencies. These serve as the smokescreen for the hidden puppet masters who operate from their financial headquarters, the City of London that occupies an area of one square mile. It operates as a sovereign state with its own judiciary, private police and has its own flag. The City of London is an economic entity which is legally separate from England and in control of lawyers and banks across the world.

Day two, titled, *The General Historic and Geopolitical Backdrop to All This* is described by David Sorensen as perhaps being the most important session of the entire Grand Jury proceeding. It exposes how an undemocratic framework has allowed the World Health Organisation to seize the rights and freedoms from the entire world population and subject nations to their tyranny.

With this awareness, it is easier to understand how a fabricated 'public health emergency of international concern' using fraudulent diagnostics along with psychological techniques of manipulation to hypnotise and brainwash the public could have happened. We can then have an insight into how 'health' is being used as the excuse for the crimes committed and to realise that true health care has been destroyed and replaced with criminal financial operations.

In the view of these oligarchs the people are livestock, which they claim to own – body, mind and soul. Testimonies from expert witnesses revealed that one of the true motivations behind the DNA altering vaccines, that are being imposed on all of humanity, is to genetically engineer mankind with a view to create a 'new model of human' that will obey these oligarchs.

Dr Fuellmich said, "Ultimately, what we're looking at is private associations, private individuals even, taking over our national governments through the World Health Organisation, using health as a crowbar to do whatever they want."

THE GRAND JURY THE COURT OF PUBLIC OPINION ON CRIMES AGAINST HUMANITY. EXCERPTS FROM CLOSING ARGUMENT BY DR REINER FUELLMICH:

Resource: Laura-Lynn Tyler Thompson, (2022) Attorney Reiner Fuellmich Crimes Against Humanity Tour.

As a backdrop – the housing crises and the resulting world economic crises has been a result of decades of looting and plundering the world's public coffers by these same players who are behind this 'pandemic' Now, they are trying to distract us from their criminal activities with scare tactics.

There was no excessive mortality until the introduction of the 'vaccinations'.

The German virologist Professor Dr Christian Drosten (who is believed to not be a professor and not a doctor) created the story that there are asymptomatic infections and that he had invented a special PCR (Polymerase Chain Reaction) test to determine who is infected. Although the PCR does not give any indication of any infection with any virus, thousands of cases were then found due to the false PCR 'test'. If the PCR had not been used then there would have been no pandemic, just a light wave of influenza.

The PCR process is not a test and has not been approved for diagnostic purposes. Dr Kary Mullis (28 December, 1944 – 7 August, 2019) who won the 1993 Nobel Laureate in Chemistry for the discovery of PCR, warned about the potential for false positives occurring and criticised its use as a diagnostic tool. He said in an interview with Gary Null in 1996, "This test does not tell you that you are sick or the thing you ended up with is going to make you sick."

As a result of the deliberate panic mongering and the corona measures created by this pandemic, it was reported to the Grand Jury, the Court of Public Opinion that more and more doctors and lawyers are recognising that democracy is in great danger of being replaced by a fascist totalitarian modal. Testimonies from psychologists and psychotherapists said that children are traumatised en-masse and ongoing long-term psychological consequences are to be expected. Small and medium businesses that formed the backbone of our economies went bankrupt en-masse and worst of all, is the damage done by the so called vaccines.

There has never been a necessity for such shots because they are based on a faulty PCR 'test' and there are effective treatments for those suffering from Covid symptoms. From the experts' testimonies, it was said that keeping your immune system intact by including practices such as eating wholesome food and avoiding junk food is important to remaining healthy.

Dr Reiner Fuellmich talked about the next step of taking legal action to the courts, stating that this is no longer possible in Germany or Canada and most judges in Europe have been captured by the Giant and its 'merrymen'. He told of the judge who ruled to 'Cease and Desist' the injurious mandates imposed on the traumatised children. The judge, the lawyer concerned, the expert witnesses and a friend of the judge were visited by the Jackboots. Just that one word conquers up a picture of the experience these people endured.

Like many warriors who have been in the fight for a long time, Dr Fuellmich 'knew' from the beginning of the announced 'pandemic' that hidden below the surface was a different story. He tells of those dear to him saying, "Do something" and he did.

We too must show up and speak up. The children are counting on it.

SHOW US THE VIRUS

> *"Leave everything you once thought you knew about viruses and disease at the door. One of the most important points to stress moving forward in our history is that viruses have never been isolated, are not contagious and do not cause disease."*
> Dr Stephen Lanka, German Virologist, 2021

South African Ricardo Marmaan's 'Show us the Virus' court case application was dismissed on 8 April, 2022 by the Western Cape High Court. This application was an attempt to stop harmful lockdown regulations, the wearing of masks, the use of poisonous hand-sanitisers and mandated injections.

The application requested that the people receive the same rights as the vaccine producers and Ramaphosa, that of legal protection. Ricardo Marmaan said that at the beginning of the process, it was requested the virus be shown. As this did not happen, he said that the South African President, Matamela Cyril Ramaphosa, was 'perpetrating a virusless pandemic against the people of South Africa'.

The case was dismissed with a punitive cost against Ricardo Marmaan.

Sally Fallon Morell MA, Dr Thomas Cowan MD and Dr Andrew Kaufman MD say in the following extract from *Statement of Virus Isolation* (SOVI), a PDF to be found at Dr Kaufman's website.

"Isolation: The action of isolating – the fact or condition of being isolated or standing alone – separation from other things or persons – solitariness." (Oxford English Dictionary).

"The controversy over whether the SARS-coV-2 virus has ever been isolated or purified continues. However, using the above definition, common sense, the laws of logic and the dictates of science, any unbiased person must come-to-the-conclusion that the SARS-coV-2 virus has never been isolated or purified. As a result, no confirmation of the virus' existence can be found. Finally, if pathogenic viruses don't exist, then what is going into those injectable devices erroneously called 'vaccines' and what is their purpose? This scientific question is the most urgent and relevant one of our time."

They conclude: "We are correct. The SARS-coV-2 virus does not exist".

A FAREWELL TO VIROLOGY

Dr Mark Bailey MB ChB, PGDipMSM, MHealSc, won an undergraduate scholarship to the University of Canterbury in 1994 and then completed his medical training at the University of Otago in 1999. He worked in many specialties as a resident doctor and a clinical trials research physician for several years and in 2016 left clinical practice due to dissatisfaction with the allopathic medical system. Dr Bailey works in team with his wife, Dr Sam Bailey and now focuses on microbiology, the existence of viruses, as well as historical and epistemological issues within medical science.

Dr Bailey's essay, "A Farewell to Virology", is based on studies and research to refute the claims that pathogenic viruses exist and cause disease. It uses SARS-coV-2 as the main example, but the principles apply to all alleged viruses. It states, "The threat of virology to humanity is increasing so it is time we bid farewell to these destructive pseudoscientific practices and free ourselves from unnecessary fears."

"A Farewell to Virology" can be found at Dr Sam Bailey's website as well as Part 2 and Part 3 of the film version produced by Steve Falconer.

The 'gold standard' scientific method for isolating and purifying is determined by Koch or Rivers postulates as follows:

KOCH (1884 – GERMAN BACTERIOLOGIST, ROBERT KOCH)

The microorganism must be found in the ill but not the healthy – the microorganism must be isolated from a diseased organism and purified – verify that the same disease is produced in the host – re-isolation of microorganism.

RIVERS (1937 – VIROLOGIST THOMAS RIVERS)

Isolation of virus from diseased host – cultivation of virus in host cells – proof of filterability – produce same disease in host – re-isolation of virus – detection of a specific immune response to virus.

A proportion of the world's population are not questioning the official narrative but it is important to realise that questions need to be asked and the science studied. One person who has done this, is Christine Massey, a biostatistician, who received her Master's degree in biostatistics from the Dallas Lana School of Public Health University in Toronto. She issued Freedom of Information Requests to government and health agencies around the world. Her request to receive copies of the records that show SARS-coV-2 has been isolated and purified has to date, come back with replies to say they do not have any evidence to say that a virus has ever been taken from a sick person, isolated, purified and shown to exist.

Christine Massey said: "It is clear there is no evidence of a supposed virus."

Ms Massey's heroic journey is ongoing and she is asking the question: "Do health and science institutions have studies proving that viruses exist and cause contagion?" She wrote in her substack (2024): "They (HIV, influenza virus, HPV, measles virus, etc, etc, etc) have never been shown to exist, clearly don't exist and virology isn't a science."

On 16 February, 2016 judges at the Higher Regional Court in Stuttgart confirmed that the measles virus did not exist. Furthermore, not a single scientific study in the world to prove the existence of the virus in any scientific literature was established. This does pose the question of what has been injected into children over the past few decades in the MMR vaccine.

Dr Stefan Lanka's writings on the historic measles trial can be accessed at the website Fluoride Free Peel along with videos such as *Pathogenic Viruses Do Not Exist* and *Virus It's Time To Go*.

PART 2
OUR SOULS ARE BEING CORRUPTED

"Everything is fine if the recipe comes from your own Book of Life but 'wo betide' you if the recipe comes from someone else's Book of Life."
Professor Dr Eucharist Bhakdi, 2023

WHITE ROSE

> *"How can we expect righteousness to prevail when there is hardly anyone willing to give himself up individually to a righteous cause. Such a fine, sunny day, and I have to go,"* 21-year-old Sophie Scholl lamented, before she was guillotined by the Nazis. *"But what does my death matter, if through us thousands of people are awakened and stirred to action?"*
>
> Sophie Scholl

Sophie Scholl was a member of the White Rose, a small, anonymous group of mostly university students who encouraged passive resistance against an encroaching fascist regime. They distributed leaflets in the hope of awakening the sleeping German population but in February 1943, Sophie, her brother, Hans Scholl and Christoph Probst were sentenced to death by guillotine for high treason.

However, the powerful words of this young warrior echo through the pages of time to bring inspiration to the hearts of today's warriors. Sophie had hoped all those years ago that people would awaken from their complacency. Today, the words of human rights activist, Vera Sharav echoed that hope in a speech given at a restaurant.

Originally, this speech was to be given at a rally in Brussels to protest the Covid mandates. However, the Belgium Jackboots stamped on the crowd, estimated to be between 50,000 and up to

600,000, threatening to unleash dogs, tear gas, water cannons and horses.

The following is an excerpt from her speech given at the restaurant on 25 January, 2022:

> *"We are at a catastrophic junction in human history. Today's predators have unleashed an injectable biological weapon designed to deliver a poisonous spike protein, and stealth surveillance technology, into the body. This weapon enables the predators to control the global population remotely twenty-four hours a day. We must choose - whether to disobey, and assert our freedom and our rights as human beings - or to be enslaved."*

Are we living in a time parallel to the Second World War?

Are we seeing the same playbook, another Hollywood drama, written, planned and performed? Absolutely.

Generations later, the predator the White Rose had experienced is alive and well. It laughs and smiles from a television set and steals the heart from the innocent ones. It now has the power to desecrate countries and even nations because it has built weapons that can destroy worlds. It destroys because it can.

The predator holds in its web those who tread lightly on the earth and the predator has spewed a poison that has tainted the soul's essence.

However, we can say, "No".

When we do, the cells of the human body begin to vibrate at a higher frequency. The power of that one word when backed by feeling and intention can conquer fear, shackles fall away, chains of bondage disappear.

When NO is said with feeling, intention and peace within the heart, it becomes a powerful force, a vehicle for the soul to smash the walls of illusion that have been built over time.

Spirit then begins to dance. The invisible tattered cloak covering the human body woven out of the threads of fear transforms into a glorious garment of light. The colours of the human spirit shine bright and its light can transform the world of the dark.

There are natural laws that govern those who carry out deadly deeds – the scales of justice are weighed and balanced. Equilibrium must be attained to bring harmony and peace. The dark agenda has created an out of balance situation and in doing so, has given humanity an opportunity to awaken to a situation that has been bubbling away under the surface for a long time.

If you take a stand, then making that stand is enough to open avenues of possibilities.

The potential to create a predator or a victim lies dormant within and can emerge to create worlds of destruction. Forgiveness is a key to activating the gifts of spirit that can support the transformation from a fall into these dark states. Lessons learnt can enhance the journey of the soul and bring awareness to the synthesis of two principals, the light and the dark. Good and evil arise from a separation from unity, which in of itself is neither good or evil.

The garb or mask that we wear may change how we present ourselves in the world. For example, masks when worn from a place of fear are symbolic of servitude, of obedience to another, speech is suppressed and those around us may take this as an excuse to bow down to weakness. When we remain strong against all odds, it can also be a gift to others to remind them to stand in their inner truth and not be swayed by forces enticing them into the darker realms.

A father said, "My child will never see me wearing a mask." I believe he was teaching his child to say 'No' when a ruling goes against that inner voice where truth is ever so softly heard. That child will have learnt by his dad's example to stand within his truth.

"Evil is something that we really need to understand. It's real," Vera Sharav said when visiting Sophie Scholl's gravesite in Munich, Germany on the commemoration of the seventy-fifth anniversary of the Nuremberg Code.

When speaking about the parallels between then and now, Vera Sharav explained how the genocidal culture existing in Nazi Germany is alive and well today. She spoke about the sixteen hundred high ranking Nazi doctors, scientists and engineers who escaped justice at Nuremberg by being secretly smuggled to the United States.

This is known as Operation Paperclip.

Ms Sharav said that these Nazi criminals were placed in high positions at major American scientific and medical centres and they continued their work. What is more, these Nazi technocrats trained a generation of American scientists, doctors and engineers. This is how Nazi methods and the immoral disregard for human values were entrenched in America.

IG Auschwitz was built as a subsidiary of IG Farben (an amalgamation of companies that had become a world leader in pharmaceuticals, dyes and chemicals) and was to be the largest wartime industrial plant. It was concluded at the Nuremberg War Crimes Tribunal that without IG Farben, the Second World War would not have been possible and a Tribunal hearing against IG Farben began in August 1947. However, there were many acquittals and light sentences given.

In 1951, IG Farben was split into three companies, Bayer, Hoechst and BASF.

Ty Bollinger (2015) wrote that Fritz ter Meer, who was found guilty of mass murder in Auschwitz, served only seven years in prison, and then he became the chairman of the board of Bayer in 1956. Carl Krauch, executive member of IG Farben and the head of the military economics for Hitler, found guilty of mass murder, served just six years in prison, and then he became chairman of the board for BASF.

Arthur Rudolph, director of the concentration camp where twenty thousand Jewish and Polish workers perished from inhumane conditions was granted United States' citizenship and went on to work for NASA. Kurt Blome, who carried out gruesome experiments on inmates was hired in 1951 by the United States Army Chemical Corps to work on chemical warfare (Wells, 2012).

Today, each of the three IG Farben 'daughter' companies is far more powerful than Farben ever was during World War II.

Operation Paperclip also captured Hollywood and Walt Disney to use sounds, imagery, lyrics and songs to disassociate and mind control children and adults.

THE JACKBOOTS

This became known as Operation Mockingbird.

Theatre, television and children's media became successful venues to create in unsuspecting minds a story the Giant and its 'merrymen' want the general public to believe. An example of this is the movie *Contagion* telling of a coronavirus scenario, with restrictions being put in place, that became the peoples' experience during the present corona story. This is known as predictive programming. Manipulating how people perceive world events so that the magician's sleight-of-hand tricks could then become believable.

Who will stop the Jackboots?

The dark agenda is now surfacing for all to see and the challenge we face is that it is global and there is nowhere to hide. Sophie and Hans' father, Robert Scholl, when sentenced to four months in prison for speaking ill of Hitler, said: "What I want for you is to live in uprightness and freedom of spirit, no matter how difficult that proves to be (Longley, 2020)."

To remain free in your thinking is a key to facing this crisis that is unprecedented in recorded human history. Trust in yourself and resist the energy of violence that is being perpetuated to create chaos and turmoil.

The white rose symbolises purity of spirit, beauty and innocence, a place of holy respite where we can heal from the activities of the everyday yang world. Bring into your everyday life, something that reminds you of purity of spirit, beauty and innocence and you will create a gateway through the dark. For example, place a picture of a white rose on a table and surround it with crystals, flowers, candles and photos of loved ones.

We may experience circumstances that are not within our control but we can choose how we respond to them and to what others may be saying.

I had the privilege of meeting Peter Legh in the 1970's. Peter had been a POW (prisoner of war) and learned that you can be mentally withered by dwelling on things that are beyond your control. So, he put his Spirit with the help of God, to support his fellow man to heal.

He wrote the following words:

ROBYN ROBINS

Offer harm to no-one
Take advantage of no-one
Treat all as yourself
Use only what you need
Give and receive all you can with love

DO NOT LET ANYONE TOUCH YOUR KIDS

"Don't ever let anyone touch your kids. Your kids are your life. Your kids are you. They are this priceless gift given by Almighty God to you as mum and dad and God expects you to look after it for him and give it back to God when the time comes. Whatever is happening in the world, the kids are yours, from God, not from governments, health ministers, not from any human being. The only one who can touch those kids is God in heaven and parents on Earth."
H G Mar Mari Emmanuel –
Bishop of Christ the Good Shepherd Church, Australia

"Never in human history have old people required young people to take risks, make sacrifices and die to preserve older people. We have a fiduciary duty to our children. Old people sacrifice themselves for children in a moral society, in a robust society, in a society that we are proud of. We do not tell children to take risks to preserve old people. We need to stand up and take a moral choice and an ethical choice for our children."
Robert F Kennedy Jr – testimony before the Louisiana State Legislature, 2021

"Our children don't care about our accomplishments or failures. Rather, they just need our presence, loving them and connecting with them, no matter what they are going through. So, take the masks off your kids, hug them and give them the human connection we all need."
Paediatrician, Dr Paul Thomas

"There will be a day, I believe, when those who have committed medical violence against our kids will be held accountable. Perhaps in their own lifetimes with persecutions for crimes against humanity but there will be a spiritual judgement. What you do matters."
Mike Adams – 2022 Propaganda Exposed, T and C Bollinger

Students in American schools such as Oakdale High School, were ripping off masks and walking out of schools with mask mandates. Having endured two long years of abuse under the banner of 'protecting them', young warriors were emerging.

I cannot imagine the hurt hearts that must flow when our warrior healthcare people witness the harming of children. Nor can I imagine the inner turmoil experienced when hearing that babies in the United States of America are subjected to a PCR 'test' at birth and if shown to be 'positive', then remdesivir is to be given for treatment.

The Hepatitis B vaccine is also given to babies, whose mothers did not test positive, on the day of their birth. These precious beings have immunity from their mothers and do not have a mature immune system. This had to be a red flag!

"Where is your heart?" asked Dr Judy Mikovits who said, "When you introduce that shot on the first day of life you will not know what epigenetic disease you set up according to susceptibility (Bollinger, T & C, 2023)."

I have heard it said that medical bioweapons have been used for the past seventy years, they have renamed them – vaccinations.

Dr Sherri Tenpenny is an osteopathic medical doctor who is regarded as the most articulate and knowledgeable physician on vaccine injuries told Dr Carie Madej in 2022 that the childhood vaccines have all been bioweapons.

For decades now, a few have fought for the vaccine damaged children and the broken families, however, fuelled by the Covid story, a new awakening is occurring.

The Gardasil jab has put youngsters with bright futures into wheelchairs.

Children's Health Defense tells the story of Merrick Brunker who was a happy, healthy eighteen-year-old before he received Merck's Gardasil HPV vaccine. Now, he is no longer physically active, cannot participate in sport and other activities, nor can he attend school and has had trouble finding work. They say that his lawsuit, filed at the time of writing by Baum Hedlund and Kennedy against Merck for knowingly concealing the adverse events associated with its Gardasil vaccine, is one of fourteen.

Bright young people are losing their careers and their lives.

Myocarditis in our young population is increasing worldwide since the introduction of the Covid-19 jab. A study carried out in Hong Kong by Li X et al, has shown that eighty-four percent of hospitalisations occurred after the second dose. As a consequence, Norway, the United Kingdom and Taiwan suspended the second dose of the Covid-19 jab for adolescents.

Dr Peter McCullough, board certified in internal medicine, cardiovascular diseases, clinical lipidology and who is one of the most cited experts in his field said that it is crystal clear that these vaccines cause myocarditis and that boys are affected more than girls. He stated that myocarditis is never mild and we have an unprecedented number of athletes dying on the athletic fields in Europe (Planetlockdown, 2022).

Dr Pierre Kory, a founding member of the Front-Line COVID-19 Critical Care Alliance (FLCCC) and board certified in internal medicine, pulmonary diseases, and critical care Medicine in his Day One opening address to the 2nd World Congress in Brazil said:

"The world has gone mad and I don't want to blame the world. The world has gone mad because it has been completely drowning in propaganda and censorship.

"The voices of truth, of science, of pragmatism are being drowned."

He said, "You know, I do feel bad for the world. I cannot stand hearing about all the people dying. They're dropping dead. Young people who don't wake up. Healthy, beautiful young people, they are not waking up right now. They are being found in cars, they're being found down in parking lots, especially being found down on their favourite places, which are the athletic fields all around the world. They are dying, young people are dropping dead, and they're sweeping them under the rug."

Doctors and healthcare workers do indeed experience the trauma of the loss of young life and of caring for the grieving families.

Paediatricians cannot miss the growing number of children with serious health issues in their practices. However, studies are now being published that may encourage questions to be asked. Dr Paul Thomas MD, FAAP, board certified in paediatrics, integrative holistic medicine and addiction medicine published a study with Dr James Lyons-Weller PhD, PE.

This study used data from Dr Thomas' practice and looked at the comparison between those who had followed the childhood vaccination schedule and those who were partially or not vaccinated. They concluded that unvaccinated children are far healthy than the vaccinated and found that the vaccinated children were going to the doctor many, many, many times fold more than the unvaccinated children to be seen for conditions such as allergy, allergic rhinitis, eczema, sinusitis, gastroenteritis and respiratory infections.

Dr Paul Thomas presented Vaxxed – Unvaxxed data to the National Citizens Inquiry on 18 October, 2024.

Dr Paul Thomas practised 'informed consent' – an ethical and legal requirement of medical practitioners saying there must be complete disclosure of risks, a comprehension of what these are and free acceptance of these risks. Being coerced, bribed or forced under duress to take a medical procedure is not receiving informed consent.

Medical practitioners who follow a government mandate of one size fits all for any medical procedure, especially one that can cause disability and death, are not practising informed consent. Dr Thomas changed the vaccination schedule according to the wishes of his patients after receiving the known advantages and disadvantages of the vaccines. Autism was greatly reduced in his practice and he said that the unvaccinated children under his care were completely healthy.

For his published work, Dr Thomas endured a successful effort to de-licence him.

ADHD was not found to exist in the unvaccinated community and this is not surprising. One of the toxic substances used as an adjuvant in vaccines is aluminium. It has been shown to affect neurotransmitters, interfere with neural membranes, inhibit the formation of microtubules in nerve cells, increase oxidative stress in cells, damage mitochondria and possibly promote DNA damage (Kennedy, 2015). These are some of the effects but not all and this list can be shared with Thimerosal that is toxic in any dose and is also an adjuvant used in vaccines. When used with aluminium, a symphony of heightened destruction may occur.

Vaccines using aluminium as an adjuvant are mandated to children without proof to say that this product is safe. On 19 February, 2019 ICAN's (Informed Consent Action Network) attorneys submitted a FOIA request asking the CDC (Centers for Disease Control and Prevention) to produce evidence of the safety of aluminium in infant and childhood vaccines. It was finally admitted that it had no documents showing the safety of aluminium in childhood vaccines. The same request was sent to the NIH (National Institutes of Health) which conceded that no records were to be found (ICAN Legal Update, 2023).

Aluminium has been used in vaccines as an adjuvant for more than seventy years. The role of an adjuvant is to enhance the immune response to a vaccine with a view to supporting stronger and longer-lasting effects. However, not all adjuvants have been proven to be safe. Dr Stephanie Seneff tells us that Dr Cynthia Nevison's research found aluminium adjuvants to be one of three toxic exposures rising in step with autism. Polybrominated diphenyl ethers and the herbicide glyphosate were the other two.

The conclusion from a paper published in the *Journal of Trace Elements in Medicine and Biology*, Volume 66, July 2021 (Shardlow E, Linhart C, Connor S, Softely E, Exley C) said, "Since aluminium is a known toxin in humans and specifically a neurotoxin, its content in vaccines should be accurate and independently monitored to ensure both efficacy and safety."

Dr Christopher Exley PhD who was Professor in Bioorganic Chemistry at Keele University and an author of the paper, wrote in his Substack the following advice when considering vaccines containing an aluminium adjuvant:

"These vaccines have NEVER been shown to be safe. These vaccines have never been shown to be effective in preventing any disease. These vaccines have NEVER been adequately regulated by any independent body such as the FDA in the US or the EMA in Europe. Until the time that all the above have been adequately addressed to the full satisfaction of both science and the public it is my advice that you should avoid all vaccines that include an aluminium adjuvant. It is my opinion that neither your life or the life of your child will be endangered in any way by making this decision. I do not come to this conclusion lightly. It is based upon a lifetime of research and a genuine fear that aluminium adjuvants underlie much of the chronic disease in children in developed nations."

Dr Exley's team is recognised as the world leader in the field of aluminium and silicon research. A passion for truth-backed science led to the story of aluminium's dark side in regards to its devastating effect on health and wellbeing. Only the Earth holds the secrets of its role when locked within the dark recesses of her womb. However, man unleashed this metal and it has found its way into every corner of our lives.

When revealing that aluminium is impacting health and contributing to, if not causing, chronic disease such as Alzheimer's, Dr Exley was faced with the dilemma of following the Giant's directive and maintaining his career status or to follow his passion, personal values and do what he believed to be true. He took the Road Less Travelled.

I believe that because of men and women of Goodwill, such as Dr Exley, the Light of the Spirit will prevail on Earth and at a future time, their work will no longer be suppressed. They will be the ones instrumental in founding the future halls of learning.

Dr Brian Hooker and medical research journalist, Neil Miller, published a peer-reviewed study showing that fully vaccinated children have a five-fold increased risk of autism compared to unvaccinated children. Unvaccinated children were found to have a much lower risk of many other chronic childhood diseases such as severe allergies, gastrointestinal disorders, asthma, recurring ear infections and ADD/ADHD.

Dr Hooker and Neil Miller also presented a study saying there appears to be a protective effect against these disorders when children were unvaccinated and breastfed for a minimum of six months, or unvaccinated and born vaginally.

When speaking on Children's Health Defense 'Friday Roundtable' on 4 June, 2022, Dr Paul Thomas said that he had approximately ten thousand patients and not one had been hospitalised with Covid symptoms and there were no deaths. However, he had two children hospitalised with myocarditis who received the Covid-19 jab on their own. Dr Thomas believed this to be 'real world data'.

He said, "Vaccines are a huge toxin that bypass the body's natural immune functions, such as the gut lining and the skin. Direct toxicity suppresses the immune system and children do not need this jab. Parents have got to wake up and do their duty as a parent to protect the children."

Neil Miller and Dr Gary Goldman published a study in 2011 looking at the United States and thirty-three nations with similar socio-economic advantages. The goal was to see if there was a correlation between the vaccines given and the infant mortality rates (IMR) of those nations. What they found was that the nations giving the most vaccines to their infants tended to have the highest infant mortality rates.

Questions that should have been asked before, are now being asked.

On 7 September, 2018 Robert F Kennedy Jr and Aaron Siri filed a complaint on behalf of ICAN against the HHS (Health and Human

Safety) for failure to answer a Freedom of Information Request to produce the records of vaccine safety assessments between the years 1986 and 2018 – Informed Consent Action Network vs US-HHS, Case 1:18-cv-03215-JMF.

The reply came back, "The searches for records did not locate any records responsive to your request."

When interviewed by Anne Vandersteel (2021), Dr Judy Mikovits said the Children's Health Defense, *The HighWire* and the Informed Consent Action Network (ICAN) have proven through lawsuits that vaccines are not safe and have not been tested since 1986. Not a single double-blind placebo-controlled safety study has been done, as required by Federal Law and none have been tested in combination for safety.

However, the vaccine story as told by the pharmaceutical companies, laid the groundwork for the acceptance of the experiment we are now witnessing. We accepted that children be injected with poisonous substances to gain entry to school, despite the fact that it is every child's right to an education. We accepted the lies that these vaccinations stopped 'deadly' illness and saved lives. We accepted the lies that they were safe and effective. We accepted the Giant's story and now they have grown into a monster called 'Covid' whose tentacles are entangling everyone in its clutches.

We put children into masks without looking to see if what we were being told is true. Those who did look, saw a different story. Maija Hahn, a certified speech-language specialist, tells us that children learn through watching and hearing and when masking the young during those growing years, speech and language development can be impacted. She said that masks may impede oral development and can influence the growth of the jaw and the mouth, which we now know affects the health of the whole body. Mouth breathing may result which can lead to long-term jaw malformations and long-term oral and swallowing problems.

Tammy Clark (OSHA Environmental Health & Safety Professional) told Dr Patrick Gentempo in 2021 that masks can decrease your oxygenation by twenty percent. She explained that we come into contact with pathogens all the time and do not become ill. However, our bodies can only tolerate a very small percentage in oxygen variation and that is four percent. When the body's ability to take in enough fresh oxygen is impacted, you are rebreathing the toxic gases that should be exhaled and you are increasing your chance of sickness.

Children and adolescents are particularly vulnerable to oxygen deficiency and the damage that can occur may not be able to be reversed.

When we mask the mouth, we are saying no to the breath of life. With each inhalation we bring Life (called Prana in India, Qi in China, Ki in Japan or Nwyfre, the Celtic term) into the bloodstream. Say "Yes" to Life – breathe.

Anthroposophical medicine sees life as a process of soul and spiritual development.

A newborn baby is like a flower that has not yet opened. This blossoming happens over the life-time. The first seven years of life are focused on growing the physical body and the childhood diseases, such as measles, mumps and chickenpox can be an important part of this process. Dr Michael Evans and Iain Roger (1992) wrote: "In measles especially, there is a profound activation of the immune system, with many antibodies produced. In the past, when children got measles, it was common for doctors to regard it as the coming to maturity of the immune system."

The body uses mechanisms such as fever and rash to release inherited miasms to inactivate a predisposition to certain diseases and to make the body a more comfortable home. However, when vaccinations stop this process, inherited tendencies are pushed into the body and can, with epigenetic stressors, surface later in life as a chronic disease.

LearnTheRisk is a website where information can be found and say, "Science is discovering there are many benefits to common illnesses, particularly in childhood." And, theorise that viruses help train the immune system in a way that helps to reduce the risk of serious issues later in life, including cancer.

The 'childhood diseases' were approximately ninety percent eradicated before the introduction of vaccinations. Nature 'knows best' and we were moving into a time when these were no longer needed within the evolutionary cycle. The introduction of health and hygiene practices, such as sanitation and clean water implementation, played a part.

Science tells us that the infectious cycle emerges, peaks, declines and then disappears. However, due to the vaccinations, when we experience a return of these childhood diseases, not in a natural form but man-manipulated, the result is a different 'beast'. We have upset the opening process of a delicate flower.

Dr Michael Evans and Iain Rodger (1992) wrote, "There is a very fine balance in the relationship between the physical, etheric and astral bodies, and illness results from a breakdown in this balance."

The body is not fixed matter but an energetic system of connectedness. The etheric and astral bodies are a part of what is now known as the human biosystem. The etheric weaves in and out of the physical, ensuring breath flow to energise and maintain overall health. To support this process, children need creative activities such as painting, dancing, swinging, singing, playing in the mud, fantasy and dreaming. Too much intellectual activity can weaken the etheric and lay foundations for chronic illness. Vaccines harden the etheric body.

The astral body is known as 'the trauma system' where vibrational imprints of our experiences that are not integrated or processed are stored.

Dr Patricia Sherwood tells us that the relationship between the etheric and astrality is critical, for the etheric acts as a buffer between the physical body and astral experiences. If it is vigorous, even if a person has a number of emotional traumas, they will not deplete the physical body. However, if it is weak and depleted, then emotional traumas vibrate directly from the astral layers into the physical body, manifesting in a range of mental and physical problems.

The soul is a fine conductor of human development – man, not so much.

Today in Western countries, chronic disease in children is in the vicinity of fifty-four percent. When I was a child, I believe it was somewhere in the vicinity of one percent. I do not remember children in ill health, except for the 'childhood diseases' that resulted in a 'fun' time of being nurtured. I remember the home-made chicken soup, bending over the basin of boiling water, a towel over my head and inhaling Friar's Balsam until a sniffling nose or chesty cough settled and breathing returned to normal. Having my chest rubbed with eucalyptus oil and best of all, my mate, Whiskey, a Scottish Terrier, to cuddle into bed with me.

To reverse the trend of chronic disease today in children is perhaps one of our most urgent challenges.

To give that beautiful flower the opportunity to grow, blossom and flourish is our job.

The template for regenerate life is to be found in Nature's Garden. Chemical farming, genetically engineered crops, glyphosate, geoengineering, to name a few, are weakening, poisoning, and destroying the natural environment to which we are intrinsically linked. The human body heals when given the right environment and so does the Earth. Nutrient dense, chemical-free, organically grown living food is the greatest gift we can give our children to ensure their health and wellbeing. Children are our future.

Indigenous wisdom may have become but a faint echo but we can re-invent a healthy knowledge base for agricultural practices and just may be, what we have thought to be lost, will again be gifted to humanity.

During the Covid time of lockdowns and mandates, the children's growing years were disrupted and they need us now to step up and say no to being forcibly injected with poisons that may maim their body and steal their life. There is no greater gift than that of a new born child. There is no time more sacred than the birthing experience. There is no greater gift than that of watching a child grow, flourish and reach their potential.

Children need us to say no to an agenda intent upon enslaving these beautiful souls in a transhumanistic world where there will be no interaction with the natural world. The children's fusion with machine will ensure that every thought, movement and bodily function will be monitored and controlled. Creativity, the forte of humanity, will be but an urge perhaps sometimes felt, but dismissed as fantasy. As too, will be the voice of the ancestors.

Mum wrote in a letter to her grandson: "Don't take this Life for granted, we pay our rent here, by that I mean, making life work for us by giving out love and our best. But, it all adds up to two things, we have a 'memory bank', no-one can rob us of our memories and second, 'your dream'. We must have a dream." I am saddened to think about a world where the children do not have grandparents to pass on their wisdom, no longer have access to their own memory bank of wonderful and loving times and will no longer have the ability to dream.

Perhaps, the children's salvation is as Dr Andrew Wakefield believes, the extraordinary power of maternal intuition. He told Dr Patrick Gentempo in 2021, "In 95 percent of families, it's the mother, that little voice inside her that says there is something wrong. And it's not an emotional issue, it's a survival imperative.

"That little voice that is there and has been for thousands and thousands of years, has evolved to become the reason we are here on earth now. Not because of men in white coats or vaccines, or antibiotics, or anything medicine has done, but because of that voice, that mother's intuition of when her baby is well and not well, what is right and what is wrong."

Dr Wakefield, a gastrointestinal surgeon and fellow of the Royal College of Surgeons, was maligned and ostracised from his profession when questioning the connection between autism, gastrointestinal problems and a link to the MMR vaccination. However, Dr Wakefield is now making films that are described as being scismic in nature. These include *Vaxxed from cover-up to catastrophe* (2016), *Vaxxed II, The People's Truth* (2019) and *1986: The Act* (2020).

Vaxxed from cover-up to catastrophe, tells the story of how published data was destroyed that revealed the MMR vaccine (measles, mumps, rubella) given at an early age posed a far greater risk of autism, especially in African/American boys. Fraudulent data was published, however, the man in charge, Dr William Thompson, known as the CDC whistleblower, kept copies of the original documents. Thirteen years later, he revealed this crime to Dr Brian Hooker, the father of a vaccine injured son.

William Thompson said, "I was involved in misleading millions of people about the possible negative side effects of vaccines. We lied about the scientific findings (Willingham, 2015)."

The CDC and health authorities hid data that to this day is causing death and heartache to many.

1986: The Act is the story of what is behind the catastrophic situation we now find ourselves in as this was the year Ronald Reagan signed the Act that gave pharmaceutical companies indemnity from damage done by the recommended childhood vaccines.

Dr Wakefield's latest film, with Executive Producer Robert F Kennedy Jr is called, *Infertility: A Diabolical Agenda*. This is a true story about a mass sterilisation agenda that took place in Africa over many years under the guise of a public health tetanus vaccination programme under the World Health Organisation.

Children's Health Defense (2022) with Dr Brian Hooker talked about the infertility issues that are increasing since the introduction of the Covid jab and tied into the infertility story is the phenomena called Decidual Cast Shedding (uterine wall shedding). Prior to 2021 there were only forty cases in open literature over a period of one-hundred and nine years. In January 2021, two hundred and thirty-six cases were reported to the VAERS system. A study by Tiffany Parotto et al, stated in summary: This survey study showed a rise in DCS experiences after the distribution of the COVID-19 vaccines.

Menstrual irregularities associated with a close connection to vaccinated individuals were also being reported. It is important for women to share their stories, however, the voice of these women was silenced and erased from social media platforms. The *MyCycleStory* (MCS) website is a place where the power of sharing personal issues and the need for research is understood.

Shedding or 'transmission' is a phenomenon documented in medical literature. In the Pfizer trial documents released by Court Order, it was recorded that they did not let pregnant women take part. No sex was allowed for five weeks after the first shot, and less for subsequent shots. If a trial participant was in a room with a pregnant woman and shared the same air or touched the skin of the pregnant woman, that had to be reported. This was noted as being a Serious Adverse Event (SAE) to the woman and the baby (life-threatening) and her progress was followed for up to six months. However, because the pregnant woman was not in the trial, Pfizer was not required to disclose this data.

It is becoming evident that the unvaccinated people are being affected and so are children. The health condition of the person in close contact with a vaccinated individual, for example, whether immune compromised or suffering comorbidities, is important as to the outcome.

Transmission through breast milk with heartbreaking consequences to the baby is also real. These 'vaccines' were never tested on pregnant or lactating women. Dr Brian Hooker said the flu shot and the Dtap shot, both recommended for pregnant women, also have never been studied on this population and recommending the Covid injection is a tragedy.

Dr Lawrence Palevsky, a paediatrician who uses a holistic approach to children's health and wellbeing told Children's Health Defense 'Friday Roundtable' on 4 June, 2022 that these vaccines show no efficacy. However, there is very damning evidence to say they are killing and maiming people. He said that newborns are presenting with strokes and blood clots. Young children are presenting with strokes, blood clots, heartaches and myocarditis and neurological problems, autoimmunity and death are increasingly evident across the age groups.

Dr Palevsky said: "The medical community and the scientific community are normalising these symptoms in children."

Dr Christiane Northrup sent out a call to women: "Wake up that Mother Bear instinct."

Perhaps it is the feminine instinct that will tilt the balance of power to defeat the Giant. When enough mothers wake to the realisation that the children are endangered then that Mother Bear instinct will awaken and that, is an unbeatable force.

If we do not stand up for our children, then we must ask the question, "Will they be strong enough to stand up for themselves?"

Following is an excerpt from a speech given by Barbara Loe Fisher, co-founder and president of the National Vaccine Information Center (NVIC), at the rally in Grant Park in Atlanta on 24 October, 2015.

> *"Those tiny miracles, God's most precious gift to us. We hold them in wonder just moments after they are born. We love them in a way we never loved anyone, and they love us in a way that no one else ever will.*
>
> *"Then, one day, we wake up. And they are as big as we are, ready to go out in the world and make their own way, and hold their own babies in their arms, completing the natural order of life.*
>
> *"But for many children, the natural order of life will never be completed. Some have already died. Some will one day join the ranks of the working disabled. And others will grow old and die in state homes, with the bodies of adults and the brains of babies.*
>
> *"For these children, the natural order of life has been forever changed by man made viral and bacterial vaccines they were required, by law, to use."*

WHERE ARE THE OLD TO LISTEN?

Where are the old to listen
Where is the buffer between old age and myself
Come back
I need you
I don't know how to grow old, there is no-one to show me
How did you do it
Who listened
Was anyone there
Come back
I am all alone
The old have gone
The young are busy
They do not see me but, I am here
Waiting, for one day
I'll be gone too
Who will say, "Come back"
I need you to listen
How do I grow old
I am all Alone

Robyn Robins – June 2009

My mum turned one-hundred-and-one in 2021. Three weeks later, she passed away from a stroke that had led to a blood clot on the brain, leaving her paralysed, unable to swallow or speak.

Mum had received two doses of the Covid-19 jab and four months later, she had passed away. She had also been given flu jabs during the time she was in the aged-care facility. Prior to this, to my knowledge, Mum had never received a vaccination, nor was she on any medications and suffered no comorbidities. It was a fall and then her inability to be mobile that preceded her entry into care. My feeling is that the 'vaccine' was the trigger that precipitated my mum's passing.

The last visit we had with her was a happy occasion and much treasured as we lived a long distance apart. Myself, my eldest son and two grandchildren filled the small room with our presence, but it was Mum who held the floor with her humour, skilfully hiding the fact that she did not remember our names. Four generations made memories that would enrich family albums for generations to come. These moments are precious milestones that warm our hearts during the times the cold winds come. And, come they did.

Months later, the whole country was in lockdown (house arrest), mandated to wear a mask, social distance and QR code to enter public buildings. Equipment in children's playgrounds was chained and schools were closed. Curfews were implemented, the distance people could travel was restricted, businesses could not function and were lost, along with income needed to provide families with the basic needs. Fear swamped the hearts of the people through the continual bombardment of horror spewing from mainstream media.

A 'virus' for the first time in the history of mankind, was threatening its existence.

When Mum turned 101 years old, we watched the occasion via zoom. She took a wheelchair ride to the community room where she was seated at a table decorated with flowers. She wore a necklace of flowers and a crown of flowers adorned her hair. Mum was cheerful and appeared oblivious to the attendees wearing what looked like hazmat suites, masks and gloves. These people gave her a birthday with care and love and it is not my intention to take that away from the individual health care workers. The everyday person was doing their best at that time. The glimpse we saw of her inmates, there for the occasion, revealed a picture of lifeless, aged men and women.

While watching, I could not help but surmise that I was looking at the collision of two worlds. Humanity in the form of Mum, colourful, laughing, joking – she was now putting a plate of cake on her head, oops – and, the faceless ones that humanity was unconsciously being coerced to become. Looking on from computer screens were family and friends, a lifetime of soul connections not able to celebrate this momentous occasion, one that will not come again.

My brother and his wife, who lived close to Mum, were 'allowed' later that day to see her through the fixed glass window of her bedroom.

Her one-hundred-and-first birthday was a repeat scenario, however, I could not access the zoom and sadly, could not partake even through an impartial screen. During the previous year, my brother and his wife were able to enter the facility, one person at a time for a short period. Influenza and Covid-19 jabs were mandated for this to happen.

During Mum's final week on Earth my brother, his wife, eldest son and a great-grandson were permitted to take turns to sit with her. Three generations supported Mum on her journey and this was a blessing. We spoke to her through telephone calls and I was told she nodded, grunted, or tried to smile.

The funeral service was live streamed. Her Queensland family gathered to watch and afterwards celebrated her life at a local restaurant. However, those who lived in her home town were masked, made to social distance and only 10 people were allowed to attend the service. The gathering of family and friends was not permitted to partake in one of Mum's favourite rituals, a cup of tea. Storytelling to begin the healing journey was not permitted.

"What about a cuppa?" Mum would ask when seeing a forlorn face. That 'cuppa' and a listening ear worked magic.

Every morning at dawn my mum would rise to hand feed a kookaburra who patiently waited on her verandah, overlooking a beautiful coastal village. On that auspicious occasion, and when the coffin was carried out of the reception area, waiting was a kookaburra.

I like to think that it was a sign from Mum to say that all was well. She had written some years before:

> "Some things have changed, but I still get excited
>
> at seeing a rainbow,
>
> however, I do not see life as coloured as before.
>
> Sunsets, I love hoping I'll see the next.
>
> The moon has lost its romance since man landed on it, but I know
>
> the evening star will always be there.
>
> When I pass, I'll slide down every rainbow and my soul will say,
>
> 'Gods in his heaven, all's right with the world', no more will I cry
>
> for the lost years."

SHE SAID

"It matters not how old you are ... but, how you are old."

We were fortunate in that Mum did not spend her last week on Earth alone and without the comforting presence of loved ones. However, many did not get the opportunity to say, "Goodbye". Stories remain unfinished and sadness will deplete those hearts for a long time to come. That important rite of passage was savagely stolen.

A countless number of the older generation spent long, lonely days, weeks and months without physical contact with a loved one – perhaps the one thing that made their lives worth living. Visits from health and social-workers were reduced or eliminated during this time. The toll on the physical, emotional and mental health was unfathomable. The injustice to our elders can never be undone.

A friend said, "Every time Mum and I were together this year, I had to wear a mask and we could only touch by elbow. No hugs or kisses. Very, very cold and something neither of us ever got used to."

During those 'hospice' times, every hug and every kiss is a momentum of love, locked away within the recesses of the heart. When the loved one passes over, this becomes a panacea within, a balm to support the pathway of sorrow. Those final months, days and moments are important and when this process is thwarted, the grieving may be prolonged and the suffering deep.

These are indeed soul wounding.

I cry for those in palliative care who were not able to say goodbye to loved ones or who were restricted in the time spent in participating in those final moments. This cruel ruling was still in place in many facilities in Australia as of October, 2022.

When a loved one is passing over, wrapping them in compassion and peace is the best gift that can be given. Everyone should be actively cared for, protected and loved during this time.

Perhaps the 'wisdom years' too were stolen from many. I say this when considering the ill health of our ageing population, something that has never been seen before. I remember elders who had sparkling eyes, walked without sticks and did not spend years in the lonely corridors of the old in a community place. Nor did they spend their days staring mindlessly at screens before being coaxed into a drugged sleep. They ate home-grown produce that bore little resemblance to the chemical-laden, genetically engineered, tasteless 'food' served today in aged-care homes. Time basking in the sun and walking on the earth was their medicine, not pharmaceutical drugs that are designed to deaden the mind and exile the spirit.

Molly moved into a large aged-care facility when, in her eighties, she became physically inactive. However, her mind remained clear and crisp well into her nineties. Her secret, she would softly confide, was to take the tablets she believed she needed at this time. However, the one given to ease anxiety and depression, she skilfully put under her tongue to dispose when the nurse had left the room. Molly said, there was not one person in the facility with whom she could have a sensible conversation and was adamant that those little pills played a major part in creating this travesty.

Psychiatrist, Dr Kelly Brogan (2019) wrote, "I learned from my own independent research about psychiatric medications: there is no scientific basis for their use. The truth is that in seven decades, not a single human study supports the idea that depression is caused by a certain kind of chemical imbalance in the brain."

Decades later, a friend who lived in a retirement village was to say she believed there was not a functioning brain amongst the residents. She asked me the question, whether it could be the copious amounts of medications they took on a daily basis. My reply was to say, "Yes, I believe these play a part." However, my friend and her husband did not have the health problems and the loss of memory issues they had after receiving the numerous jabs and the swabs of the Covid era.

I cry for the loss of elderly life before its time and especially during the Covid story. One fact to come out of the 2022 Grand Jury the Court of Public Opinion was that in some areas, patients in care homes whose immune systems had been weakened by the jabs were subjected to infections. This happened because ill people were transferred to care homes to allow hospital space for the arrival of patients with the Corona 'virus' that never happened. Therefore, many immune depressed elderly passed away from infections that would not normally be introduced into their environment. Aged-care staff were not equipped or qualified to offer the care needed in these circumstances.

I cried when hearing professionals speak of the elderly in their practice who had quality of life before receiving the Covid-19 jab and are now fighting chronic illness. The toll this takes on the family and those close is enormous. Time making happy soul enriching memories is cut short.

I cry for the young who one day may say, "Come back, I need you to listen, how do I grow old, I am all alone."

"When the Grandmothers Speak and are Listened to the World will Begin to Heal"

A HOPI PROPHECY

"Have courage for without it we have no justice, without justice, we have no freedom and without freedom, we have no peace."
Beatrice Longvisitor Holy Dance – Oglala Lakota – The Grandmothers' Wisdom

My maternal grandmother passed away when I was six years old. I remember her telling me fairy stories, Tinkerbell was the favourite. I remember standing on a hill above the town where we lived and looking at the flickering lights that she insisted were fairyland, and to me they still carry that magic.

My paternal grandmother is remembered for having a healing herb to soothe all ailments.

I write children's stories and have a love for the natural way of healing. We do carry the grandmother wisdom within the cells of our body.

Mum took myself and three children to live with her when there was nowhere else to go. We turned a garage into a flat that soon began to resonate with children's laughter and became a witness to those tears silently shed when no-one was watching. The elderly neighbours took us into their hearts, it was that elder wisdom that held us while we healed.

Phoenician, Egyptian, Roman and Gnostic teachings tell of Sige, the Grandmother of Creation, the Silence before the Word. Sige says, "Profound is the silence before action."

There is no other time in recorded history when the Grandmother Wisdom is needed as it is today. It is time for Sige to break her silence for within her essence lies the wisdom of the ages, the collective voice of the Grandmother. She must now rise to stand against the present-day tyranny to protect the innocent.

I am witness to the breaking hearts of grandmothers whom I know. Grandmothers who were not 'allowed' to see precious grandchildren due to heartless mandates that have no scientific basis. Grandmothers who wisely chose not to be part of an experimental procedure, were told that they could not hold, kiss or cuddle their grandchildren.

I spoke to a grandmother who told me that her young and healthy granddaughter suffered myocarditis after receiving the Covid jab. Chemotherapy was the 'prescribed answer' when a cancer diagnosis followed and now, this lovely flower is wilting. The positive to be found here is that others around her are choosing to make a more informed choice with regards to the ongoing vaccination schedule.

A grandmother whose heart is breaking when witness to a beautiful healthy grandchild receiving toxic vaccinations from the day of her birth. Being a witness to the child's health deteriorating to suffering from 'Covid' and still receiving ongoing injections during that time of being ill. This grandmother is now holding the fear for future health issues that the child may experience.

Soul wounding, fear and trauma are ongoing as children are being maimed and losing their lives.

MADDIE DE GARAY

Maddie de Garay was twelve at the time her mother enrolled her in the Phase III clinical trials that Pfizer conducted at Cincinnati's Children's Hospital in Ohia.

Within twenty-four hours of receiving her second Pfizer jab in January of 2021, Maddie was hospitalised with a severe reaction, experiencing symptoms that included gastroparesis, nausea, vomiting, erratic blood pressure, and memory loss.

Today, Maddie is in a wheelchair, is tube fed, suffers daily seizures and other ailments.

Neither Pfizer nor any other regulatory body have reached out to the family. Indeed, after numerous visits to various medical professionals and hospital admittances, they were told that Maddie's problem was anxiety.

Dr Henry Ealy, who is donating time to assist Maddie, told Jonathan Otto that the family support is likened to running a marathon and then the next day, running a marathon and then, the next day, running a marathon. He said you have to run that marathon to give them a chance and if you do not, then there is no chance and all hope is lost. He said that there is no help and no accountability.

Experience, love and compassion are what is needed now for this community of injured people that is growing every day.

Attorney Aaron Siri is representing the family and this story of courage and the brutal cover-up and dismissive behaviour of the regulating health agencies can be found at his substack.

Maddie's story is not a rare occurrence but highlighted because it is a part of the Covid story. Parents for decades have 'run the marathon' with no end in sight and in a lot of cases, little in the way of medical assistance.

We do need to be aware that there are risks with these experimental shots with little or no financial assistance from the government or medical agencies and becoming increasingly so, no insurance coverage.

Former Black Rock Executive Portfolio Manager, Edward Dowd, told Robert F Kennedy Jr, "There's an industry that's been defrauded. It's the insurance industry. They are currently paying for excess deaths due to a product that kills. And they're gonna be paying for years of disability from vaccine injuries. I don't think they're gonna put up with that once they realise what's happened (Marks, 2022)." At the time of writing, some insurance companies are saying that this is a medical experiment taken at the person's own risk and therefore, equivalent to suicide.

Prior to 1986, parents were receiving compensation and the pharmaceutical companies were concerned at the increasing payouts. However, since the National Childhood Vaccine Injury Act of 1986 giving them no liability for their products, those who were vaccine damaged found the claim compensation process to be extremely difficult. Parents who experienced the heartache of seeing children lose the ability to live to their highest potential, have been screaming into deaf ears for decades. Many have been 'running the marathon' for a long time.

Dr Rashid Buttar chose to run the marathon and was one of the first to question the Giant's Covid narrative. He believed that we were in a battle for mankind and successfully treated many people who had been given little hope for survival by the allopathic medical system. His message to these people removed panic, anxiety and fear and restored faith and hope.

When speaking to Dr Bryan Ardis about the censorship he and others were experiencing, Dr Buttar said, "They don't want anybody that has a message of truth and power showing people that they have the power within themselves. They don't want that message to get out because that empowers individuals."

Dr Brian Hooker, the father of a vaccine-damaged child, chose to work with a heartbreaking scenario, to run the 'marathon' every day and at the same time, use his skills and knowledge to make a difference to the lives of other people. Polly Tommey is Programme Director of *Children's Health Defense TV* and the producer and director of documentaries that reveal the extent of vaccine injuries and the tragedies of affected families.

Being the mother of a vaccine-injured son was Polly Tommey's catalyst to become a support to millions around the world experiencing a similar journey. Barbara Loe Fisher, co-founder and president of the National Vaccine Information Center (NVIC), has for decades led a movement to educate the public on vaccine injuries and deaths. Her journey welled from her son's injury following a vaccine and her deep dive into the research available at the time.

Dr Andrew Wakefield's journey from losing everything to bringing awareness to the darkness happened because a mother of a vaccine injured child asked for help and he listened.

It was Ty and Charlene Bollinger's tragic loss of loved family members that sparked their mission to embark on a journey of discovery to prove that cancer is not a death sentence. Today, the movement they began has not only given us a road map to health and wellbeing, but I believe, also brought awareness to the dark side of the vaccine story. This was so successful that President Biden announced twelve of these esteemed warriors to be the 'Disinformation Dozen'. Based on a report published on 24 March, 2021 by the Centre for Countering Digital Hate Ltd (CCDH), it was proposed that these twelve 'anti-vaxxers' are responsible for sixty-five percent of the anti-vaccine content circulating on social media platforms. These are: Joseph Mercola, Robert F Kennedy Jr, Ty and Charlene Bollinger, Sherri Tenpenny, Rizza Islam, Rashid Buttar, Erin Elizabeth, Sayer Ji, Kelly Brogan, Christiane Northrup, Ben Tapper and Kevin Jenkins.

Could the intimidation and harm directed at these warriors have been an attempt to 'silence' those questioning the official narrative, an attempt to silence free speech?

I was a witness to the effects from Western methodology when sharing my dad's journey through the cancer diagnosis, treatment and passing over and the loss of my daughter to the mental health system. This resulted in my passion to find a better way that led to years of research.

However, a soul's journey is sacred and because there are often higher reasons for choices made, I have also come to learn to accept what is and to strive to be free from judgement.

We must also remember that our legacy of being a living, breathing man or woman is a gift.

The concept of 'woman' or 'man' is today shrouded in confusion, the result of an agenda carried out by the Giant and its 'merrymen' to psychologically lobotomise the human being from its soul essence.

The journey of a woman from maiden to mother to crone symbolises the three stages of womanhood – the sacred journey of the goddess. My friend Don, who is a gay man, tells me that our 'great work' is to bring new life into the world and he says that is something he will never experience. It is deep within the womb that the secrets of birth are hidden.

The wise grandmother knows she is the keeper of the family grail, the cup of wisdom and knowledge passed down through the generations. She is one face of the crone, the traditional overseer of birth, death and rebirth.

And when the grandmothers speak, it is time to listen, the healing will then begin, Hopi prophecy tells us.

THE FARMERS' REVOLUTION

*"All of us are born to be heroes.
We all have the divine seed of courage and justice
planted inside of us. Let's do it."*
David John Sorensen, 2022

In July 2022, the new war horse, the tractor and heavy farm equipment, rumbled across highways and byways in the Netherlands. Farmers and ranchers came together to protect their livelihoods and farms that have been in families for generations. For weeks, farmers in the Netherlands engaged in protests over their government's plan to halve the country's nitrogen and ammonia pollution by 2030. An estimated thirty thousand people took to the streets, cutting off highways, torching bales of hay and spraying government buildings with manure.

The mainstream media portrayed this as an environmental issue, misrepresented the protesters as extremists, or it was simply ignored.

However, evidence is mounting that a mega-city is proposed for the Netherlands where people will be fed by 'vertical farms'. These are industrial food growing sites run by Artificial Intelligence (AI) and using genetically modified produce to grow the amount of food required to feed the densely packed populations.

Breggin and Breggin (2022) reported that the Netherlands is the second-largest exporter of agricultural products, with estimated exports of 104.7 billion euros in 2021. Only the United States exports more agricultural products. Given the size of the Dutch agricultural production, the Dutch government's plan will expand the current food crisis and further dependence on new agricultural systems such as industrial and Artificial Intelligence-driven vertical farming.

In October 2022, Dutch farmers threatened more protests in response to the government's call to seize by force up to six hundred farms they claim to be the heaviest nitrogen emitters. They are saying that nitrogen is a pollutant and not a fertiliser that plants need to grow and thrive (Huff, 2022).

Many were beginning to realise that the Giant and its 'merrymen' have slowly but surely undermined the ecological systems of Earth. The soil, nature's health-giving sustenance, is being sabotaged and debased to become an artificial product devoid of the life-giving nutrients that humanity needs to thrive.

In an interview with Russell Brand (2022), Vandana Shiva explained that we do face a serious ecological crisis, but one caused by industrial agriculture. She said the same system that is pushing an anti-people, anti-life, anti-nature agenda shaped a system that is causing the problems. Forced on people through regulation are systems that support a dark agenda.

Farmers are a victim of this system. However, their call for 'help' was heard and truckers, fire fighters, fishermen and people from everywhere responded. The movement swept into Germany and Switzerland where posters of the 'most wanted' (such as Klaus Schwab) were displayed around the city. The movement swept the world and grew day by day.

The anti-life agenda that Vandana Shiva speaks about has been a step-by-step project. While we slept, our land was denatured with chemicals, glyphosate being one of the most-deadly and that is now well documented. Dr Don Huber, Professor Emeritus, Purdue University said, "When future historians come to write about our era, they are not going to write about the tons of chemicals we did or did not apply. When it comes to glyphosate, they are going to write about our willingness to sacrifice our children and to jeopardise our very existence by risking the sustainability of our agriculture – all based on failed promises and flawed science. The only benefit is that it affects the bottom-line of a few companies." (Mercola, 2011).

Genetic engineering is an anti-life project that has been forced on food production, animals, nature and humanity. Jeffrey Smith, a renowned researcher on the dangers we could be facing, tells the tale in his books, through his website and his tireless lectures. Ho (2013) said, "Artificial genetic modification is crude, imprecise, and interferes with the natural process." An unfolding story told by independence researchers is pointing to adverse effects to health and longevity, the ecosystems that support life and a nightmarish situation being left for generations to come.

We bought the story that these methods were necessary to feed the world.

We bought the story that natural farming methods could not feed the world's growing population. In fact, as I write, a large percentage of the world population is fed by food that is grown by natural farming methods.

We bought the story that there were too many people in the world.

It is time to reclaim our right to grow and eat health-giving food – to reclaim our right to Life.

Geoengineering (the artificial modification of Earth's climate systems) is an anti-life project and Dane Wigington from *Geoengineering Watch* believes that there are now virtually no natural occurring weather patterns. He says, "The very essentials needed to sustain life on earth are being recklessly destroyed by these programmes."

Those chemtrails we see criss-crossing the skies are spraying our planet with anti-life substances such as nanoparticles of plastic spiked with beads of aluminium. Advanced nanoparticles of plastic are found in our food and water. They can be found in increasing amounts in our body and the first study to show evidence of microplastics in the human placenta was published in Environmental International in 2021.

Aluminium, barium, strontium, manganese, polymer fibres and others are being dispersed by aircraft all over the world. Our major oxygen supply comes from plankton found in the oceans and this has been severely disrupted as has the natural rhythm of the water cycle. Approximately seventy percent of plankton, the building blocks for marine life, is reported to be lost.

Mum wrote about the legacy her grandfather left: "You made me see the grey skies as beautiful white clouds rolling over the Bay, see the white horses hitting the rocks and the gulls in flight, retreating from the storm. I was never afraid again. How boring were the trees? You showed me that there were three-hundred and sixty different types of gummies (eucalyptus or 'gum trees' that are native to Australia) and not two trees the same. You made me aware of the sunsets setting over the Bay in all their splendour and sinking below the horizon in tranquillity. We watched the dying embers of a coal fire with pictures to see. Laying on our backs, we would find the pictures in the clouds. What a marvelous legacy you left me."

She loved to reminisce about how he taught her to look up at the night sky and to pick out the constellations, the planets and to marvel at the moon and the twinkling stars. Have we lost this simple sharing and the passing on of knowledge to our young? It is sobering to wonder if the clouds we are seeing today are nature's creation or artificial constructs and whether those twinkling stars are man-made satellites. The anti-human agenda is, as Vandana Shiva said, anti-life and it affects creation.

Fluoridation is an anti-life agenda. The fluoride put into drinking water is a byproduct of the phosphate fertiliser industry. It is a toxic waste containing other contaminants such as lead, arsenic, mercury and more. There are studies to show that it is linked to increased bone fractures in children, arthritic-like symptoms in adults, lowered IQ in children, the lowering of melatonin production and the early onset of puberty (Connett, Beck, Micklem, 2010).

According to William Fischer (2000), laboratory studies show that low doses of fluoridated water can cause serious genetic and chromosomal damage to plants, animals and humans. Lynne Farrow (2013) wrote that fluoride's ability to displace iodine is another concern as iodine is needed by every cell in our body for optimum health and plays a crucial role in breast health. Fluoride fatigue is real according to Dr Bruce Spittle (2008) and shows up as fatigue, headaches, muscular weakness, skin rash, mouth sores, depression, nervousness and dizziness.

Dr Dietrich Klinghardt's (2020) work revealed that elements damaging and even deactivating our pineal gland are aluminium, glyphosate and fluoridation. It was found that electromagnetic frequencies open the blood-brain barrier to allow these to enter.

Rene Descartes (1596-1650) philosopher and mathematician, called the pineal gland, the 'principal seat of the soul'. Ancient yogic teachings describe the pineal gland as a physical centre connecting to the place of wisdom, intuition and to higher fields of consciousness.

The pineal gland has a strong antioxidant and anti-inflammatory influence and has an important relationship to the circadian rhythm. There is scientific evidence to show the relationship between its calcification and disorders such as melatonin deficiencies, mental illness, ischemic stroke, neurodegenerative conditions, sleep disorders and the ageing process (Chlubek and Sikora, 2020).

Scientist, Barrie Trower told Dr Reiner Fuellmich (ICIC.LAW) that electromagnetic frequencies have been proven to penetrate the blood-brain barrier, allow neuro-toxins in the blood to cross and cause neurological symptoms – a person can either die or become seriously impaired.

Electromagnetic frequencies can enhance human life or depending on the frequency used, can be an anti-life agenda and this is the scenario we are faced with today. We ignored the warnings of scientists such as Dr Neil Cherry, an associate professor of Environmental Health at Lincoln University in New Zealand who extensively researched and lectured on the detrimental effects of electromagnetic radiation on the human body.

The author of *Cross Currents, The Body Electric* and a Nobel Prize nominee Dr Robert O Becker who said in an interview in the year 2000 with Linden Moulton Howe, "I have no doubt in my mind that at the present time the greatest polluting element in the earth's atmosphere is the proliferation of electromagnetic fields."

The information contained in the *Seletun Scientific Statement*, published on 3 February, 2011 by a group of international scientists known as the Seletun Scientific Panel, led by Professor Olle Johansson PhD. It recommended that new exposure standards were urgently needed to protect long-term public health worldwide (International Electromagnetic Fields Alliance, 2016).

The BioInitiative Report 2022, the work of a group of international scientists, an update of a report published in 2007 and covered thirty years of scientific studies revealed the evidence of harm from electromagnetic frequency exposure. Of particular concern was the detrimental consequences to our most vulnerable, the young and the developing babe in-utero.

We are ignoring the warnings given by present-day scientists who have devoted decades to studying the effects of these frequencies on life on Earth.

Dr Martin Pall PhD, Professor Emeritus of Biochemistry and Basic Medical Sciences at Washington State University, is a published and widely cited scientist on the biological effects of electromagnetic fields and speaks internationally on this topic. He said in his Special Report on 5G, published in 2018, "Putting in tens of millions of 5G antennae without a single biological test for safety has got to be about the stupidest idea anyone has had in the history of the world."

When talking about the devastating effects on life when cell phone towers are turned on, scientist/author/journalist and environmentalist, Arthur Firstenberg, tells us that this is happening now with 5G, only this time instead of blaming an influenza virus, society is blaming a coronavirus.

He wrote in 1997: "This is an urgent plea to environmentalists and to those within the telecommunications industry, to doctors and business people and government officials, that microwave radiation is an imminent danger to all of us more or less equally, and that for our common survival we must immediately halt the expansion of wireless communications upon this earth. There is no greater threat to our common future."

Meanwhile in Australia, vehicles of all descriptions displaying billboards are travelling to country towns and cities in an endeavour to educate the people on the true Covid story and the upcoming food supply issues. Known as the Billboard Battalion, it is a grassroots movement also aimed at 'calling out' the media who they say, "Have absolutely no integrity, no honesty, and are totally committed to telling lies and spreading misinformation as the official propaganda unit of a government and bureaucracy who are in the business of costing peoples' lives and causing our country irreparable damage."

The Giant's agenda to remove family and privately owned farming businesses and place these into the hands of the multinational corporations has been unfolding as we slept. Legislations and policies have been covertly introduced that have changed the face of farming forever. We are witness to the 'finale' land grab brought about by events that have been deliberately orchestrated.

I spoke to a young man who was heartbroken because he could not afford to continue the farm he grew up on, that had been in his family for three generations. The cattle that roamed freely on green pastures could no longer provide a living for his hardworking farmer parents. The costs involved in maintaining such a property were now beyond their reach.

The small town cushioning this farm and many like it was exploding with incoming populations eager to settle into the newly built housing estates. Infrastructure to support this growth had not been put into place. He reminisced about his growing days, the bus shelter the community had come together to build and many similar projects.

When a lad, he said he would never have dreamt of vandalising his home town or doing anything to bring disrespect to his elders. He confided that even with two full time incomes, he and his wife could not afford to buy a home and so had decided not to bring children into a situation where they could not give them a nurturing experience.

When witnessing the children of friends growing up in day care centres, he said that this was not an experience he wished to give children of his own. He remembered having a 'mum at home', being free to roam in nature, milk a cow, climb a tree and swim in a nearby creek. Perhaps he was mourning the loss of being able to pass onto the younger generation the art of being a 'boy', growing in Nature and learning to become the man who can fulfil the task of supporting family and community.

The young woman whose heart held a similar story because the farms surrounding that of her parents' property were transforming into housing estates. The loss of the citrus orchards growing on the rich red farming soil in this area can never be counted.

The woman speaking of her husband's bravery in beginning his own carpentry business in a large town, his heart aching for the land he knew and grew up on. The fish farming business they had operated for many years was now gone due to the soaring costs of maintaining such a venture. Taking their bounty to the central fish market as had been the case for many years was no longer a viable option. "Mum and dad farming," she said, "was now gone."

Indigenous cultures believe that the land is sacred and does not belong to anyone, it is a gift to us for a short time.

However, power has been given to the Giant's 'merrymen' that can now lead to farms being confiscated, animals and crops destroyed, businesses closed. As for the backyard garden, it could be a distant memory. In my growing years, our backyard vegetable garden complete with pecking chickens, ducks and geese was a favourite place to sit and dream. I remember foraging through the shell grit in the chicken pen for bits and pieces to make into jewellery.

Watching with fascination when my dad prepared a chicken for our Sunday lunch. When it was done, the chicken that had graced our yard, happily picking at seeds and insects would now be given the honour of being the centre-piece on a table covered with a white starched cloth, carefully ironed serviettes, crystal glass and silver cutlery. Crunchy, steaming hot potatoes, pumpkin and succulent peas, freshly picked that morning from the garden, would decorate the large crockery platter.

I remember Mum bustling around the kitchen and then, hearing the sound of a knife slicing onions. The making of the seasoning was a meticulous affair and she called, "Would you pick the parsley, dear?" I would wander into the vegetable patch and, being careful to ensure that no-one was watching, pick a tomato from the bush laden with ripe, red balls. Wiping the bounty on my dress before devouring its succulent fruit. I can still close my eyes and see the splendour of home-grown vegetables and herbs, the chickens and geese wandering the yard unafraid, the deed done, life goes on. Later that day, hands would fold into a gesture of prayer and gratitude for the gifts given us and to honour the chicken's life, well lived.

Nothing was taken for granted in our family.

However, events leading up to the corporate take-over of our farming culture have been unfolding for a very long time and the voices of those enduring the injustices have not been heard due to not having a platform from which to speak. This is changing as we are now facing the demise of farming systems that have sustained humanity for a very long time.

What will we eat?

Facilities are now in operation to breed genetically modified bugs to feed the masses who are told that these are 'good for them and the Earth'.

Anyone for 'fake' meat?

According to Wade Northausen from Billboard Battalion, we have a small window of opportunity to stop the dark path we are sleep-walking down. He is a third-generation farmer who has been in the 'fight' for a long time and his interview with Maria Zeee is one every Australian needs to hear.

When speaking of the work Billboard Battalion is doing, Wade Northausen said people generally were receptive to hearing what they were saying, especially those who had lost loved-ones to the Covid jab. However, many had no idea that there are alternative media platforms.

Amish farmer, Amos Miller, the owner of Miller's Organic Farm, Pennsylvania, is fighting back and has endured a long six-year legal battle, hundreds of thousands of dollars in fees, unlawful visits from the Jackboots and a threatened gaol sentence for providing nutrient-dense food employing traditional farming practices. Dell Bigtree interviewed Amos Miller on *The HighWire* in 2022 where he talked about the nutrients given by healthy soil to cows who in turn give medicinal milk products. This in contrast to the industrialised raised animals and produce and the possibility of resultant disease.

Amos Miller asks, "Is this food production safe?"

Many are asking the same question including the safety of fruit and vegetables grown in soil enriched with agriculture poisons. Australian Farmer, Bev Buckley (2010) said that most agriculture poisons used extensively in the industrialised way, leave residues of breakdown chemicals when they degrade and, in some cases become even more toxic.

It is Ms Buckley's opinion that the epidemic of diseases we are seeing today is caused by this pollution and the solution is not in more man-made drugs but in growing healthy nutrient-rich food. She tells us that healthy food does not attract pests, insects and diseases that are nature's way of ensuring unhealthy plants do not reproduce, the fact that farmers need to use these substances with such frightening frequency is a clear indication that the food they are producing is not healthy.

Amos Miller said, "It is so important to learn our children how to be farmers – keep the family farms alive."

Where I live, there used to be many dairy farms and now, only one Australian owned, fourth generation farmer remains. Here we can purchase 'bath milk' from grass-fed cows and goats and locally grown produce. However, over the years, this farmer has fought hard to maintain this icon, at times having to pay fines for selling quark made from raw milk and eggs from chickens free to pasture. I have seen here the birth of a calf and its loving welcome into the world by the midwife farmer, and its anxious mum. The soft green grass and the warm red soil cradled its frail body, the sun's warmth bestowed a welcome blessing. I had witnessed the miracle of life.

When I was a child, we piled into the car on Sundays to drive to the outskirts of Sydney to visit farms offering fresh vegetables, cream and milk straight from the cow. We would pick blackberries on the side of the road and my dad would make pies to go with that cream. I remember picking mushrooms growing wild in the paddocks under the welcoming gaze of the farmers. Wandering through a walnut orchid and taking home a bounty. These farms have now become housing estates and the sides of the roads are sprayed with glyphosate.

However, I have the memories forever held in the photo album within my heart centre.

THE JACKBOOTS

On Sunday mornings, I drive to our local organic market where herbs, fruit and vegetables picked the previous day can be found. Best of all is having a chat with the farmers who grow the food. During the lockdowns, masking, closed borders and all the Covid-induced fear, these people endeavoured to ensure that the restrictions did not interrupt the supply of health-giving food. Their promise was that they would do everything in their power to ensure that this was so and even under difficulties, this was fulfilled. Here, people gather, music is played, laughter and chatter can be heard, children climb trees and the atmosphere of 'being human' has become a place of light and refuge.

This to me is a blueprint for the world to come and that is what I hold within my inner vision.

The farmers at this market grow living, health-giving food. Despite the obstacles, these farmers support the soil to be rich in nutrients and sustenance to grow vegetables, fruit and animal produce to nourish the body, mind and soul. There are pockets of farming communities around the world endeavouring to do this and these too are our heroes.

Farmer's Footprint is an example, exposing the human and environmental impacts of chemical agriculture, offering a path forward through regenerative farming practices free from industrial methods and a return to The Garden of Eden. They are a coalition of farmers, educators, doctors, scientists, business leaders and the founder of this movement is Dr Zac Bush.

Dr Zac Bush is board certified in internal medicine, endocrinology and hospice care, an international speaker and educator. His broadcasts teach about the microbiome's relationship to health, disease and food systems, he educates on the role of soil and water ecosystems in human genomics, immunity and gut-brain health. Dr Bush founded Seraphic Group and Project Biome.

He said, "We need to be in the dirt together. We need to look to mother earth as our template."

The Australian link to *Farmer's Footprint* says: "By re-establishing our connection to nature and re-discovering our relationship with the living earth, we can make healthier and more harmonious decisions around what we eat, where our food comes from and how we care for our country."

Japanese farmers said that the ties between the soil, the people and the web of life were disabled on that fateful day in 2011 when experiencing the Fukushima Daiichi Nuclear Plant disaster. The farmers, however, continued to sow despite an uncertain future amid enormous contamination that can remain for tens of thousands of years. They said that this is even more reason to seek the way to an organic future.

And, this is the way of farmers worldwide who love the earth and all living creatures. These 'men and women of steel' continue to sow knowing that they are the backbone to a community relying on them for sustenance and the maintenance of health. Farmers today are fighting for the freedom to continue this legacy.

PART 3
CREATING A NEW WORLD

The soft gentle flow of my voice bubbles like a brook
I remember a time when my voice was heard
It was a long time ago
Why do I cry
I cry because no-one hears me
I cry because I am alone
I cry because you do not know me
I am Gaia
Hear me before it is too late
Hear me speak

Robyn Robins

LIFE WITHOUT FEAR

> *"The good news is that you are in control of your health destiny. The bad news is ... you are in control of your health destiny. Your body responds intelligently to what you perceive, believe and intend more than to what is "really" happening, so if you are fearful, conditioned into a victim mindset, and expectant of continued patterns of negativity, you are more likely to have continued negative outcomes. Without fear, your body can do what it does naturally – recalibrate and become whole/healthy again. In this way, fear is the sickness, and your symptoms, their duration and severity – are the expression of your fear."*
> Kelly Brogan, 2019

A world where freedom and human rights are respected may seem like a dream but the 'old' world is not working, dissipating before our eyes and opening the way for pioneers to step forward with innovative projects.

As dense city chaos increases, many are moving to less populated areas, finding freedom and resettling where joy, fun and excitement can be an everyday experience.

Joy, fun and excitement dissipate fear.

A reconnection with nature dissipates fear.

We were given a narrative that was fear-driven and joy, fun, excitement and a connection to nature almost disappeared. Those whom we love may have become distant, perhaps carrying misguided beliefs that fostered polarisation. Life-giving freedoms such as speech, the ability to support self and family and to choose health care options were threatened. The narrative, designed to dehumanise, traumatise and to take away hope was a powerful 'spell'.

However, those changes to our lives, and more, were not brought about by a 'virus', but fear.

Robin Sharma (2021) wrote, "Fear works like this, I have found. Run from it and it will come closer to you, with even more force. Go directly toward it and it will turn to go, like an uninvited guest who realises they should not have shown up." He goes on to say that keeping fears in the basement will brainwash you into believing they are vicious, but go down the steps, turn on the light and look them in the eye and they will look like cartoon characters.

Fear is nothing but an illusion created by the manipulation of our mind.

Fear in the heart changes our biology.

Dr Masaru Emoto, the author of *The Hidden Messages in Water*, demonstrated how water crystals are affected by the environment, by emotions, feelings, thoughts and words. Humans are water beings and when uplifting vibrations such as joy, laughter and happiness flow through our system, health is the outcome. However, when expressing the lower vibrations such as anger, hopelessness and fear for a prolonged period of time, our body can spiral into a diseased state.

Humans as crystals of water need the elements, fire, earth and air to remain balanced and whole. We have been indoctrinated to believe that the sun is dangerous (*slip* on a shirt, *slop* on sunscreen and *slap* on a hat), walking on the earth is dangerous (wearing shoes made of synthetic fabrics prevents this connection), breathing air is dangerous (wear a mask).

I grew up surrounded by a small backyard vegetable garden, ducks and chickens. There was always a dog, a cat or both. My brother and I roamed with the neighbourhood children, having little in the way of toys but buckets of imagination to invent our own fun. We swam in the nearby river, climbed trees, rode billycarts and we were never bored. Mealtime was a family occasion as were regular picnics with grandparents, aunts, uncles and cousins.

Best of all, we had 'cracker night' which was a celebration of Queen Victoria's birthday, held on 24 May each year. Pocket money was saved to buy the precious bounty such as jumping jacks, tom thumbs, skyrockets, Catherine wheels and sparklers. My dad built a bonfire in the backyard and excitement mounted as the event drew near. On the night, neighbours arrived each with their own box of carefully chosen fireworks, we called 'crackers'.

When I was a teenager I was fortunate to have a group of friends who would get-together on a regular basis to talk, laugh, dance and sing. In other words, I grew from a child to an adult having no fear of nature, the sun, the air, the water and most of all, other humans. This is a blueprint that I inherited for health and wellbeing.

It is time to consider the blueprint we would like to hand our children to sustain them through the years of living to ensure they are able to stand strong and resilient, like bamboo, when dark clouds drift across the clear blue skies.

Children in the Western world are locked into a cycle of endless competition within the school curriculum and recreational activities. Dr Bruce Lipton reminds us that cooperation drives evolution and the Garden of Eden is the height of cooperation between species, it is not a battleground.

The Darwinian theory is wrong, said Dr Lipton, a stem cell biologist and a recipient of the 2009 Goi Peace Award. His discoveries in opposition to the narrative that life is controlled by genes, gave rise to one of today's most important fields of study, the science of epigenetics (Otto, 2021: Vaccine Secrets, Reloaded).

Are we raising our children to create a battleground? If the answer is 'Yes', then how do we turn this around and guide them towards a pathway where they will have an awareness of how important it is to recreate the Garden of Eden? The blueprint is already in place, we have just 'messed it up a bit'.

When we stop the poisoning of the earth, water and air that has occurred through the many mechanisms the Giant and its 'merrymen' have engineered in order to control and change creation, Nature will know how to re-create abundance, peace and balance.

Dr Masaru Emoto said that we must stop being agents of destruction, become agents of revival by healing the land, the rivers, the oceans and the planet in its entirety. The answer is a return to the circle of Life – the circulation of resources, of water, and of Life. He says that this is our responsibility as occupants of this delicate and crystal-like planet.

Perhaps, that is what our inner being is aching to once again be a part of – a return to nature and a return to our spiritual self.

An important step to take is to not be overwhelmed by the dark clouds engulfing humanity but to breathe and, then, take one step at a time or as Dr Tom O'Bryan tells us, one base hit at a time wins the game. Begin by educating yourself and become aware of the reality that will become our future if we remain in the dark. If we do not know that a problem exists, then how can we change it?

Do not persuade friends and family, live your truth and if people are interested, they will ask questions.

Ask yourself the question: "How can I be part of the solution?"

The next step is to put in place a daily routine that supports strengthening and healing. Trust in your body, your ability to thrive and be a part of creating a time-line that has a very different look to the fear-based, surveillance/transhumanistic agenda. Disconnect where possible from the current system of control, for example, reduce a dependence on technology and vote with your money by supporting locally produced products. Shop at farmers markets and get to know the people who grow your food and how it is produced. Use cash wherever possible.

Turn off the television knowing that it is a vehicle for propaganda and is compromising your integrity. Turn off the lies. Do not surrender to what you know is not your personal truth. Do not compromise your conscience to an oppressive regime.

Find your tribe – like-minded people who support your values.

Live in alignment with freedom.

THE JACKBOOTS

Do not let others intimidate you into wearing a mask or participate in an experimental procedure with no scientific or medical validation. Do your own research, listen to your inner intuition and then, you can make an informed decision.

The Giant's agenda is creating polarisation and chaos. The choice here is to give in to the fear and become like plasticine to be manipulated by powerful outside vectors, or, to know that we have the ability and the power to create systems to support a society far removed from the dark direction we see unfolding.

Ask the questions:

"Do I believe in my body's ability to protect me?"

"Do I want to be a part of the transhuman movement?"

"Do I want to live in fear?"

"How do I want my life to look going forward?"

Many have asked these questions and the answers they have received have led to putting into place a new way, a better way founded on freedom and the honouring of human rights.

A masterful magician, the Giant has planted seeds of fear and only we can decide whether to water these or let them remain dormant. Getting together face-to-face with others willing to discuss the things that are unsettling is a place to begin to defuse a fearful narrative.

Dr David Hawkins' work on calibrating human levels of consciousness revealed that 'fear' resonates at a very low vibration. Fearful thinking can affect others and can infiltrate the collective mood, leading to powerlessness and victimhood. Acceptance, on the other hand, resonates at a higher consciousness level and is not interested in 'pointing the finger' but is dedicated to resolving issues and finding out what to do about problems.

We experienced what it is like to live in fear when the Covid restrictions were put into place and many recognised the subtle undercurrent of fear that has haunted our everyday existence. Is it possible that by accepting 'what is' and coming together to seek resolutions to the resulting chaos, we are on the pathway to moving into a higher consciousness and a more balanced and loving way of living and being?

A RETURN OF THE SOPHIA

HEALING THROUGH LOVE AND WISDOM

The substance that nurtures our body
The radiance of our human soul
The wisdom in our spirit
Our deepest inspiration
Eternal Sophia
Clothed with the Sun
Crowned with the Stars
Creating the New Earth
A place of compassion
Of healing and of justice
For all living beings
Your day of the return is now
Arise and flourish within each of us
So within and without, the earth becomes your throne
Dr Patricia Sherwood PhD, 2007 Holistic Counselling a New Vision for Mental Health

Sophia personifies healing through wisdom, the recovery of the wholeness of the human psyche. Dr Patricia Sherwood says, "Sophia has been in exile from mainstream life for generations and her exile has broken our connection between body, mind and spirit."

In the Pfizer documents released under a Court Order, they found that in 2021 Pfizer assured the FDA that they were hiring twenty-four hundred full-time employees to deal with the flood of adverse effects they knew would come. This was based on the adverse effects they had already seen. An appendix to the Pfizer document titled Cumulative Analysis of Post-Authorisation Adverse Events Reports revealed nine pages of 'Adverse Events of Special Interest' (Public Health and Medical Professionals for Transparency, 2021).

You may ask why you have not heard this information in mainstream media. That is because of the media blackout we now have in place all around the world. If you speak out against the narrative with facts, you are banned from social media and silenced.

At the time of writing, we do not know what we are dealing with as full disclosure on the Covid-19 jab ingredients has not happened. It appears that ingredients differ within batches and that some may be a placebo and others to varying degrees contain toxic substances.

However, doctors and scientists from around the world are working to support those who have been injured and many are having success in alleviating symptoms and reversing harm. These practitioners agree that the body heals itself when given the right tools and that healing comes from acts of love, heart to heart listening, sharing a comfortable silence. The Mum who kisses a grazed knee. They know that healing does not come in a bottle, a pill or an injection.

This is the gentle way, healing through wisdom as personified by Sophia, the feminine aspects of our nature, long in exile. Perhaps, a gift from Covid is that the imbalance in our health system is coming to the peoples' awareness. The harsh, ineffective male dominant way, force and control, has consequences that are now being revealed. It is time to embrace the gentle yet fiercely passionate way, healing through wisdom.

This is the Sophia, the feminine spirit working with nature's pharmacy to bring the body to a place of balance in order to restore health and wellbeing.

The Sophia, a metaphor for healing with wisdom, also represents an aspect of the feminine that is an intrinsic part of every human, whether male or female. It is the courage to stand behind our convictions by honouring the spirit within. It is the mother bear instinct that Dr Northrup speaks of and it is the strength to make those decisions that honour our truth whatever the cost may be.

Jonathan Otto (2021) said: "Are you taking the vaccine of the mind through movies – the news where indoctrination is happening? Our souls are being corrupted."

The Giant virtually 'owns' the media worldwide, including magazines, newspapers, medical journals and the publishing business. Therefore, scientific studies must be well scrutinised for authenticity. Studies showing effective treatment for Covid-like symptoms are rarely, if at all, reaching the final publishing process.

Only the official narrative is permitted and only the official treatment protocol is permitted.

Medical Totalitarianism was put into place over a long period of time and is the cornerstone to the Giant's agenda. The 1950's was a time when corporate business was birthed on a large scale and I was an unaware witness to the infiltration of pharmaceutical companies into Australia.

What is now a concrete jungle, when I was growing up in an outer suburb of Sydney, was gentle suburbia, fibro houses adorned with flower gardens and a hand-weeded lawn. A vista of market gardens stretched as far as the eye could see. It was here that Lebanese families tilled the soil and peddled door to door, their freshly picked produce. Home-made billy carts flew over a dirt footpath surrounded by scrub that hid many a secret cubbyhole. That changed when Pfizer bought the farm land and Nature's medicine garden became a synthetic, 'pill in a bottle' manufacturer. Luxurious office space, factory and warehouse facilities became the view.

My mum suffered six years of agoraphobia following a traumatic time nursing her own mum, my grandmother, until she passed from cancer. There were times when Mum could not go to the letterbox and yet, one day she walked out of the front door and applied for a job in the factory when local protests were lost to Big Pharma. This was the year I began my High School education.

I do not know if this was a regular occurrence, but one day, the workers on the assembly lines were asked if they would participate in a 'drug trial'. Mum put up her hand. The small group of volunteers were given the pills to take over a short period of time and then were requested to document any effects. Everyone, without exception, experienced symptoms, all except Mum. And, she was the only one who had not been given a placebo!

The nocebo effect is well documented in medical literature. In indigenous culture, 'pointing the bone' is a long-known phenomena and the modern-day version is when a diagnosis is made, the harsh chemical treatments fail and the patient is told to go home and put his or her affairs in order. The patient can be left without hope and the doctor's prophecy can become self-fulfilling.

Perhaps taking a pill that had never been tested and asked to record symptoms can also trigger a 'nocebo phenomena' but what about Mum's result in this 'trial'? Maybe there were no effects to this medication, or none that affected my mum over a short period of time. Or, as family members have suggested, knowing my mum, she just ignored them.

Her voice echoing through time said, "It's mind over matter, you know."

How did my mum walk out of the house into the work-a-day-world at a time when mothers with families who entered the workforce were frowned on by many?

She said, "I believe that my grandfather's words were what made the difference. I repeat over and over, in life Lass, there are only two things you can do – you can quit or you can carry on."

She was to say, "The thing I have learnt from being agoraphobic is to never be afraid of a single human being, not a child, woman or man, we are all special, we are all human."

When I entered the workforce in the 1960's, I applied for a secretarial position in the marketing section of a pharmaceutical company. I remember the gold-plated desk plaques that were presented to the local doctors when introducing the new 'wonder' drugs. On the wall in the canteen was a dispenser filled with the latest antibiotic that anyone could access when suffering a sniffle or feeling a 'bit under the weather'.

The underbelly was slowly creeping into an innocent period in Australian history. We were dazzled by plush office space in which to work, executives in designer suites fresh faced and bushy tailed after a period of training at the parent companies in the United States. We were promised a panacea to our physical and mental ailments.

How did medicine change from the plant-based system that supported the healing process to poisonous petroleum-based chemical compounds? When did health and healing morph into 'Big Pharma'? Ty Bollinger (2016) said, "We have to go back to a paper published in 1910 called the *Flexner Report*, which dramatically – and for all intents and purposes, permanently – changed the course of Western medicine.

"Powerful corporations and the AMA hired a man named Abraham Flexner to conduct an assessment of 155 medical schools throughout North America. Flexner evaluated the various teaching methods used at each school in order to compile and establish the standardised system of medicine that his bosses wanted to come to fruition."

Tried and true medicine could not stand the onslaught of propaganda and big dollars.

Dr Darrell Wolfe told Ty Bolinger (2015), "By 1925, over 10,000 herbalists were out of business. By 1940, over 1,500 chiropractors would be prosecuted for practising quackery. The twenty-two homeopathic medical schools that flourished in the 1900's dwindled down to two in 1923. By 1950, all the schools teaching homeopathy were closed."

Based on the *Flexner Report*, colleges teaching these healing modalities as well as osteopathy, nutrition and holistic, functional and integrative medicine were forced to close. The very profitable but toxic petrochemicals that have numerous side-effects replaced nature's living medical system. Natural medicine could not be patented and therefore, had no place within the medical monopoly the AMA, powerful corporations and the publishers of the report, the Carnegie Foundation, envisaged.

Funding was cut for herbal remedies and some such as Cannabis were demonised. Many bought the package and today, we are seeing the breaking-down of this medical system. I have heard a doctor say that after all those years of work and cost, it was to realise that he had learned a very sophisticated marketing system for promoting the pharmaceutical industry.

Captured also was the rite of passage called 'birth'.

Grandmother wisdom carries ancestral knowledge that is passed on through tribal elders when a maiden becomes a mother. However, this sacred time was also brought under the Big Pharma umbrella and morphed into a clinical medical procedure. Doctors in white coats brandishing needles became the welcoming committee for the new born child.

Anxious mothers strove to become the 'modern mum' armed with the latest scientific findings. The grandmother wisdom that had evolved over millennia receded into the mists of a past, now gone.

There has never been a more important time to take your health into your own hands.

Study the work of those courageous doctors and scientists who are releasing information that can be life-saving. Build your own medicine chest to suite your needs and budget.

There is a lot you can do to bring health and wellbeing practices into your daily regime.

Many of these are gifts from Nature.

It is time to reclaim our medical freedom and then, a smorgasbord of tried-and-true remedies will be at our disposal and we will have the health that for a long time has been but a dream.

THE BEST VACCINE EVER INVENTED

Maintaining the miraculous symphony of body, mind, soul and spirit is the best vaccine. Our whole body is in constant communication within itself and the environment to maintain health, balance and aliveness. However, supporting the body to become attuned to health and wellbeing is met with many obstacles in today's toxic world. Some of these stressors are:

Genetically modified food, fast food, food grown with chemicals and chemically laden water

Radiofrequency radiation and electromagnetic frequencies

Toxic chemicals

Emotional stressors

Vitamin and mineral deficiency

Injectable toxins, heavy metals, parasites, nanoparticles and synthetic biology

Magnetic fields, power lines and incorrect wiring prevent our homes from breathing

Listen to the body. Symptoms, such as fever, pain, trembling and anxiety are the body's way of saying that there are stressors to be dealt with and it is doing its job. However, like no other time in recorded history, has there been so many issues to deal with and, when the body becomes overloaded, then we are on a slippery slope. Chronic illness can be the result. For example, when subjected to a constant bombardment of stressors, one final trigger, such as a toxic injection can lead to chronic illness or even death.

Stress depletes the immune system. If you believe the Covid narrative, then the resulting stress can lead to a less healthy and vital immune system. Our biology was never meant for chronic stress.

The trick is to become aware of the toxic stressors. Aim to eliminate them as much as possible from your personal environment, one step at a time so as not to create another stress. Know the protocols that are free and abundant to bring into your everyday life that can make an impact on health and wellbeing.

SURYA THERAPY

The most valuable way of getting Vitamin D is from the sun and can also be found in fruit and vegetables grown organically, free from chemicals and manipulations. Surya is the Sanskrit name for the sun, known and worshipped as being the bringer of life. Every living organism on this planet relies on the sun for life, health and vitality. We have been misguided into believing the sun is something to fear.

From the sun we receive nutrients and living energy to sustain our physical body to be vibrant, healthy and confident. Spending hours under artificial light can deaden our vitality and our spirit. When in the sun, our body is designed to only take in what we need, however, this process can be hindered by toxic chemicals, electromagnetic frequencies and heavy metals, to name a few. We need to become aware of this in-order-to implement safe practices such as not basking in the sun when the sky is riddled with chemtrails.

Expose as much of the body as possible during 'sunning' times, free from toxic sunscreens and clothes designed to block the sun's healing rays. My children enjoyed 'sun kicks' whenever possible from a young age. It is time to make 'sun kicks' fashionable again.

Connecting to natural light is important for our physical, emotional, mental and spiritual wellbeing to support cleansing, healing, balancing and to ensure that the light we shine is bright.

Traditional Chinese Medicine advocates the best way to receive the sun's healing benefits is by direct skin and safe eye exposure. When the light from the sun enters the body through the eyes, the pituitary gland and the pineal gland are activated, assisting in the regulation of body functions such metabolism, immunity and endocrine balance. Spending long days indoors under artificial lighting and the prolonged wearing of sunglasses can hamper this process.

All hours of sunshine are valuable for different purposes.

The hour before sunrise and sunset are known as the 'hours of power'. These times are important in preparing for the day to follow and the night's rest to come.

HONOUR THE DAY

Consciously greet the sun upon rising, allowing its light to set your daily rhythm and this will become a practice that will be an important part of your daily health routine and bring many benefits.

An example of my morning routine is as follows:

Upon rising, I drink a glass of spring water into which I have squeezed the juice of a lemon. This supports the body to clear the toxic build-up from the night's rest, a time, when our body regenerates and heals.

Moving to a grassed area, I allow my bare feet to touch the earth to receive her healing touch. I give gratitude for the gifts received and to the sun's rising beams of light that activate my whole being in preparation for the day. When the body flows with nature's rhythm, we too flow with the essence of the grace bestowed on all creatures.

Following the morning yogic blessing, I move into gentle poses to awaken and realign the whole body. This does not have to be a long process, a routine of five or ten minutes is beneficial. This time spent focusing on nature, your breath and body with awareness and joy, is more important than spending that time in angst thinking about the busy day to come.

The yogic Tree Posture is a favourite as I am aware of the importance of balance, especially as you age. I chant a mantra, 'Om Ah Hum'.

Humming has been shown by science to assist in clearing the nasal passage that is a first line body defence. Hum and your body's wisdom will adjust to a frequency to bring balance, peace and healing.

I retire to my meditation room, light a candle and move into floor asanas followed by a little breathing, meditation and prayer. Again, this need only be for a short period of time such as five or ten minutes of mindful practise.

"Base hits when done repeatedly win the ball game," says Dr Tom O'Bryan (2016).

BLESS THE DAY

At the end of the day, the sun kisses the earth before slipping over the horizon. Night stealthily covers the earth and its creatures with a soft dark orange blanket that prepares us to drift into the world of dreams. However, when exposed to the blue rays of technology during this time, the natural process of falling into a healing sleep can be disrupted. Blue light disrupts the natural circadian rhythm and is emitted by digital devices such as LED lights, cell phones and laptops.

This is a time to journal, pray and give gratitude for the events of the day.

A time to keep electronics to a minimum as the bedroom is not a place for them. Sleeping in a dark room with no flickering lights, televisions, mobile phones or electric clocks is important. Ideally, cut the power to the rooms in your home that do not need electricity as electromagnetic radiation interferes with the body's ability to detox, heal and rebalance. The time of sleep is when these processes are activated. Not eating at least three hours before retiring is advised as the body needs energy to heal during this time.

NATURE'S PHARMACY

Trying to heal without nutrition is like building a house without raw materials.

Raw food contains the highest amount of nutrients.

Grow a kitchen garden, even a herb in a pot on the verandah will give health benefits and grow in alignment with your vibration to produce a medicine that is solely for your own body.

One of life's joys is to share a home-cooked meal with family and friends as this replenishes the heart. Growing food and sharing with others is a soul enriching experience. Food is a major part of the medicine story to bring healing to the body, heart and soul.

Mum said that if you grow a plant, then you will always have a friend.

It is important to purchase locally grown, in season produce and question whether this is so because the body needs the seasonal nutrients to align with the changing of the seasons. Eating out of season may throw the body out of balance. When eating with the seasons and flowing with the cycles of nature, we can lead healthy, peaceful lives.

One of my healing protocols is called Essiac Tea. This particular blend of herbs is grown in a local organic nursery from seed nurtured by the sun, rain, wind and earth. The spirit of the plant, alive and well when carefully hand picked with intention and packaged with care. I then put my healing spirit into the blend when adding the herbs to water, stirring and bottling to become a tonic I take each morning and night with gratitude. Human and plant wisdom combined can create an alchemical process that is not found in artificially produced products.

Organically grown fruit and vegetables are the platform on which to base your healing protocol. Supplements as advised by your health-care professional may include the following that are recommended in many regimes to assist healing from the effects of Covid illness.

Vitamin A – Can be obtained from fresh organic carrot juice.

Vitamin C – Found in vegetables, fruit and abundantly in citrus fruit, natural Vitamin C is vital for maintaining a healthy immune system.

Dr Archie Kalokerinos MBBS PhD FAPM wrote the book, *Every Second Child* in which he refers to the fact that in the area where he was working, every second indigenous child either experienced death or injury as a result of vaccination and poor nutrition, especially when being low in Vitamin C. He fought for the wellbeing of Australian aboriginal children, administered Vitamin C to the communities before vaccination and reversed some vaccine reactions by giving Vitamin C intramuscularly or intravenously (Scott-Mumby).

Intravenous Vitamin C is a valuable treatment and Dr Thomas Levy said, "In a nutshell, unless the patient has advanced organ damage and is very near death, intravenous vitamin C, in sufficient doses, can always be expected to save the patient from succumbing to an advanced infection."

Dr Levy says that the Riordan Clinic in Wichita, Kansas has clearly established the safety (and efficacy) of even the highest dosing regimens of vitamin C on a routine basis. Over the past 32 years, more than 150,000 intravenous infusions of vitamin C have been administered at Riordan campuses. Doses have varied and no significant adverse side effects have occurred, and no kidney stones have resulted. For more information on the vitamin C-related research and results, visit the Riordan Clinic website (*Orthomolecular News Service*, 2022).

Quercetin – can be obtained from eating organic onions, apples, blueberries, green tea, grapes, dark leafy greens and the rinds and skins of plants. Quercetin can assist to correct disturbed light frequency.

A family story remembers the time my dad had whooping cough when a youngster. My grandmother placed white sheets over the windows in the room he was in and bowls of sliced onions around the room. She replaced the onions regularly and stayed with him until he recovered.

Breana Lai Killeen wrote that the *Los Angeles Times* printed an article in 2013 saying, "In a sickroom you cannot have a better disinfectant than the onion. It has a wonderful capacity for absorbing germs. A dish of sliced onions in a sickroom will draw away the disease – they must be removed as soon as they lose their odour and become discoloured, and be replaced by fresh ones."

I wish my grandmother's knowledge had been recorded.

Quinine recipe: The peel of three grapefruit and three lemons (must be organic). Cover with good quality water to three inches above peel and simmer for three hours. Strain and keep in a mason jar. Take 2 tablespoons twice per day.

Zinc – Eat plant foods high in zinc, such as seeds (quinoa, hemp, chia, pumpkin), legumes (lentils, black beans), nuts (pecans, pine nuts), mushrooms (shiitake, white button), grass-fed beef and oatmeal.

Garlic – press cloves of garlic and allow to stand for fifteen minutes – good medicine.

SAVE SEEDS

Save seeds and take the most fundamental step towards health freedom.

"When you control seed, you control life on Earth," said Vandana Shiva, a world-renowned environmental activist, food sovereignty advocate and feminist.

Vandana Shiva, the founder of Navdanya Research Foundation for Science, Technology and Ecology (India) and President of Navdanya International received the Right Livelihood Award in 1993, regarded as an 'Alternative Nobel Prize'. Her books include: *Earth Democracy: Justice, Sustainability and Peace* and *Stolen Harvest: The Hijacking of the Global Food Supply*.

Situated in North India, Navdanya is an organisation that has evolved to protect biodiversity, the Earth and small farmers through the knowledge of non-violent farming. It promotes chemical-free agriculture, an awareness of the dangers of genetic engineering, fights against patents on seeds, stands up for seed sovereignty and the peoples' rights to food and water security. Navdanya says that organic agriculture is not just a source of safer, healthier, tastier food, it is an answer to rural poverty, saving the Earth and the people.

When a seed is cradled in earth and can receive raindrops, sunshine and air, magic happens. One tiny seed can then alchemise into a plant.

Mathew Evans (2021) wrote: "It turns out, a seed is more than just a seed. A seed is a mini-universe. As well as the energy reserve to get it started – the carbohydrate and fat locked inside its germ – each seed also has its own microbiome, its own microbial signature, an entire genetic code along with the seeds' own DNA, that allows it to burst into life."

A seed carries the 'memory' of the plant kingdom's lineage and is a powerhouse of light and Life. The genetically modified seeds that Bayer/Monsanto have inflicted on the world do not carry this living energy.

"We have a higher duty to protect life on Earth, to protect the biodiversity and to pass on seed to our future," said Vandana Shiva.

THE BEES

Bees found refuge in my brother's barbeque.

Their fate in the hands of many would have been an indignant attack with a weaponised substance designed to annihilate such pesky creatures. Instead, they found a home in a beehive and flourished. Today, my brother and his wife are beekeepers with many hives, supplying family and friends with scrumptious honey.

This honey is included in my health regime and I believe this to be medicine the like of which can never be found in a chemist shop. Nature's pharmacy holds a bounty that we have only begun to explore and understand.

Bees give us wax to make candles that have been shown to assist in clearing a polluted and an electromagnetic frequency ridden home. Bees give honey, known to have many health benefits and medicines such as bee pollen, royal jelly and bee venom, an ancient and safe medicine. Propolis has antimicrobial properties, has been shown to be neuroprotective and is a powerful addition to any healing protocol.

Lucy Cavendish (2019) wrote, "The Druids believed the bees come from the sun, and that the creation of mead is the transference of solar energy into liquid gold ... and through that liquid gold we alchemise life, vitality, industry, love and sweetness."

Bees as pollinators have a vital impact on the food chain.

The bee community is highly organised and self-governing with each member working in harmony. The bees bring many gifts including a blueprint for building a harmonious and sustainable colony. They come together to get the job done when necessary and so much we.

ABHYANGA

Part of my weekly routine is to massage myself from top to toe with organic black sesame oil for approximately thirty minutes. I sit in the sun (as naked as possible) or lie on a yoga mat or bed swathed in towels. This is known as abhyanga, an ancient Ayurvedic full-body massage to assist with the healing and detoxification process. It is a time to play relaxing music and to enjoy the moment while the skin absorbs the qualities of the oil. I have found this to be an excellent health tool to calm the nervous system and to assist my skin to repair from the damaging effects of toxicity. I then languish in a warm bath to which I add Epsom salts or hop under the shower, visualising a waterfall washing away toxins and dead skin as well as mental and emotional debris. Being in the shower or bath is grounding and as-a-consequence, insightful ideas, thoughts and messages can pop into my head. An Epsom salts foot bath can be a gentle alternative to draw out toxicity.

FOREST BATHING

Shinrin-yoku or forest bathing is a science studied for many years in Japan. It is regarded as preventative medicine because it has been shown that spending time in a forest environment has a positive effect on our body-mind experience. Just being in such a place with awareness, known as mindful forest therapy, is a de-stressor and can benefit heart rate, blood pressure and blood flow to the brain. Trees release aromatic chemicals said to have anti-cancer properties. Spending time in such an environment can boost the immune system and the effects are lasting.

Beth Kempton (2018) says that the medicine of the forest is far more than a contemporary wellness trend. People have lived in forests since ancient times. Nature is in our blood. It is in our bones. It is in our very human spirit. It is the haunting call of the mountains and the swirling pull of the sea, the whispering of the wind and the secrets in the trees.

When visiting a forest setting, have an awareness of nature's pharmacopoeia and know that within its pages lies the secret to eliminating the sludge from modern living. Nature's library holds a treasure trove of information, every tree a book of knowledge, each leaf a wise word, if only we had the ears to hear and the eyes to see.

GROUNDING/EARTHING

When the skin touches the earth, nature's healing remedies are absorbed into the body and can neutralise natural waste from the body's metabolic process to maintain health and balance. Today, however, the body finds it difficult to cope with the bombardment of artificial toxicity that comes from many sources such as medical diagnostic equipment, household appliances, electric power lines and microwave radiation. The cells begin to lose their light, metabolism is slowed and human tissue begins to deteriorate. People in past cultures did not have these problems, they wore leather footwear, slept close to the earth cocooned within her heart beat and were grounded.

When connecting to the earth, the chaotic sea of energy we are continually bombarded with is transformed by nature's wisdom.

Symptoms of not being grounded can include feeling angry, frustrated, rejected, light headed, anxious or mentally mulling over past events. Eating raw organic food, walking barefoot on the earth, gardening and touching the living soil with your hands can be ways of staying grounded. If connection with the earth is not possible, wear red sox as colours vibrate to different frequencies and red resonates to the part of us that connects to earth.

Earthing supports the immune system, is scientifically known to bring the stress hormone cortisol into balance, can enhance sound sleep and is essential for health and wellbeing. Barefoot contact with the earth after hopping off an airplane can work wonders for softening jet lag woes. After running a marathon, take off those sweaty shoes, step onto the earth to accelerate recovery and relieve muscle tension. Being still and sitting with a quiet mind will connect us to the electromagnetic pulse of the Earth and we then may receive nature's wisdom that can assist to counteract the effects of harmful electromagnetic frequencies.

Walking on sand, diving into a wave, allowing a tinkling brook to flow over your feet or sitting barefooted in your garden with feet touching the earth are ways to assist the body to maintain a state of balance. Spend time near the sea where the four elements, air, earth, fire and water combine to bring about healing.

Grounding mats can now be purchased and are a wonderful tool to add to your healing protocols.

The foot contains an intricate network of nerve and acupuncture points. Applying pressure to a part of the foot to free blocked energy and bring relief to another part of the body is well documented. This is known as reflexology used by many ancient cultures such as the Indian, Chinese, Egyptian and North and South American healers. Mother Earth is a wonderful reflexologist, so take off those synthetic shoes, walk barefooted and allow her to do what she loves, work with your body to bring healing and balance.

MEDITATION

I found an article on Clifford Carnicom's website that resonated with my years of experience when working with the practices of relaxation and meditation.

Leslie Oliver wrote, "Thus, rather than my body forming an obstacle waiting to be hit, the meditative state allows the electronic waves to pass THROUGH my body without harm." It was explained that when the body is solid, these waves slam into it, creating pain. However, when in a relaxed, unfearful state of mind, we are less solid, lighter and more open.

I believe that decades of running yoga classes gave me 'real world' data that I can now draw upon with a different understanding.

The system of yoga I implemented was to bring together gems of learning from different modalities. This evolved around creating a meditative state, commencing with asanas (postures) carried out in a slow manner with awareness of body and breath. I learnt that slow, gentle movements were the secret to releasing trauma and toxicity. The meditative state would deepen as the class progressed to breathing and meditation, followed by a relaxation such as the classical yoga nidra.

I recorded many of these practices on tapes for my students and received feedback that they were used on a frequent basis and especially during times of stress.

Over time, I witnessed healings taking place and I witnessed the coming together of people to form strong bonds of friendship that they were to carry with them for many years.

I am not saying that these successes were the result of the classes but I am saying that they played a part. It makes sense to me that when we are relaxed, our bodies are in a state of flow allowing discordant frequencies to pass through. When in fear or anger, we 'freeze' and become like a block of ice ready to 'fight' off the 'virus' or whatever we deem to be attacking us.

Someone said to me, "There's always something out there ready to get us!"

What if we changed that story (which is what it is) to one that says there is nothing in organic Creation that is not supporting the human to flourish and survive? That would be a very different way to live our lives.

Bringing meditative practices into our everyday life can be a major player in how we navigate these tumultuous times. Yoga, Kum Nye, Tai Chi and Qigong are examples of avenues to explore. However, quietly sitting in a place in nature and dropping into the heart, fishing and watching the ebb and flow of the water, gardening, painting, handicraft, pottery can all be avenues to explore to 'just be' and go within.

LAUGHTER MEDICINE

In my years of teaching yoga, I have not given the following exercise without everyone rolling on the floor laughing. I often had a picture of myself laughing and no-one joining in but it did not happen. Happiness is a natural state of being, so getting into the habit of laughing is a great idea. Resulting from this practice, I have seen deep belly laughter which is something we have almost forgotten how to do.

Laughter 'turns on' positive switches in our bodies and floods our cells with feel good chemicals that lift our vibration and press the 'heal' button. People laughing, whistling and singing is a childhood memory that makes me smile to this very day. It has been said that five minutes of laughter can activate the immune system and this positivity can remain with us for up to twenty-four hours.

Laugh, whistle and sing to turn on the 'heal' button.

This is soul medicine. If those dark wings of fear come flapping, no matter how hard it seems, take your awareness to something beautiful, a flower, a picture, the falling rain, whatever makes you smile. Something I do at these times is to walk barefoot in nature and consciously feel the sun's warmth filling those dark holes of despair. Remember, you can do this in your mind, you can always smile, chuckle and yes, even laugh, no matter what.

LAUGHING YOGI MEDITATION

> *Kneel on the floor, bring the toes together and separate the heels. Lower the buttocks to rest between the feet. Alternatively, you may sit in a chair. Yawn, stretch your arms over your head and then bring your hands to rest on the knees. Remember to use slow conscious movements.*

Release any tension and tightness by rotating your awareness around the body, breathing into each part and letting go.

Inhale while gently drawing your shoulders up towards the head. Feel the tension in the shoulder and neck area and exhale as you return your shoulders to their original position.

Smile and bend forward from the waist, bringing your forehead towards the floor. Smile and feel your body smiling. Say, "My body is smiling," and slowly return to a sitting position.

Chuckle and bend forward from the waist. Chuckle and feel your body chuckling. Say, "My body is chuckling," and slowly return to a sitting position.

Laugh and bend forward from the waist.

Laugh with your body and allow laughter to flow into every cell in your body, let go, laugh with abandon, feel the whole body laughing.

BREATHE

When faced with a stressor, our breathing becomes restricted. Become aware throughout the day of your breath and take a moment to become conscious of your body posture and your breath. Straighten your body, soften the body and allow the breath to deepen. Taking the time to breathe with awareness can change a frantic rhythm to one of inner calm which in turn will assist the oxygenation of the blood and increase energy flow.

During times of experiencing grief, follow the Breathing Meditation but instead of breathing into the belly, identify the place in the body where the sad feelings are pronounced. Breathe into that part until feeling relief and repeat this on a regular basis.

Breathing Meditation: Breathe well to live well.

Lie in a comfortable position (or sit in a comfortable chair), your feet flopping out to the sides and your palms facing upwards. Gently close your eyes and move your awareness around the body, consciously inhaling into each part holding tension, letting go with each exhalation. Feel yourself becoming more and more relaxed and rest in the calm stillness, the place where your inner physician resides.

Let go of body awareness and become aware of your thoughts. Allow them to flutter across the screen of your mind like a flock of birds flying across the sky. Have no involvement, watch them come and watch them go. After a time, take your attention to feelings or emotions and allow the sensations to rise and dissipate.

Now, become aware of the natural breath – the gentle inhalation, the exhalation and flow into the pause at the end of the breath. Breathe slow and deep into the belly and allow it to move freely as the breath flows through your whole being. Become the silent witness, watch the body being breathed.

When you are ready, let go of breath awareness and become conscious of the room you are in, the sounds within the room, the sounds outside and stretch and stretch. Curl up into a foetal position, give yourself a hug and give gratitude for your body, your breath and your life.

IT IS AN ART TO LISTEN WITH THE HEART

Be still and listen. Sit in a comfortable position, close your eyes, become aware of your breath.

Let go of the awareness of the breath and take your awareness into the heart centre.

Listen.

Be still and listen.

When you are ready, become aware once again of the breath, open your eyes, place your hands in a prayer position, touch the heart and give gratitude.

When we practise going to this place within, this can then become a part of our everyday interactions and may give us the ability to remain centred in any situation.

Acupuncturist, Peter Crook, wrote, "Become more aware of your thought processes and the quality of listening you give to another, in fact, to any sound. Our heart can hear deeply without the interference of thoughts in the mind, giving a deep feeling of resonance and understanding."

And, he said, "How can one tell that you are listening to your heart and not just following your thoughts? Listening with your heart has feelings and is felt with your whole body, an inner soft feeling of righteousness. We will often say, 'That just feels right. There's no doubt.' When thoughts move there are words in your mind or head and in you, it will make sense, has logic to it, or, there will be the feeling that a decision has to be made."

Today, voices are bombarding our senses with different points of view, with propaganda, with subtle manipulations and on it goes. By taking the time to be 'still' and to bring awareness to the heart's wisdom, we can navigate chaos and confusion and no longer be buffeted by the winds of anger or fear.

Swami Dasma-Mata Arunya (1994) wrote, "The quiet mind is not acquired, it is simply developed when we are inspired by inner conviction be it philosophical, religious or humanitarian. When we are motivated by ambition the 'quiet' is smothered by noise and confusion, greed and, often as not, dogma."

In 2006, she wrote, "Each one of us has the intuitive capacity to KNOW when something is being offered with Love and to realise that just because lots of people support something or someone, it may not necessarily resonate as true for us."

And, "Discernment is not judgement, for it comes from a place of inner knowing that is not processed through the rational/intellectual mind. This does not mean that something may not be right for others, or that it has no right to be happening, just that it is not something we choose to support at that time."

Create a sacred space within your home – use scarves, crystals, candles, flowers, sacred images, drawings or personal objects with meaning. Over time, when being in this space to just be, to meditate, pray, draw, hum or to gently move the body, it will become a place where you will feel safe, a place to go to listen to the heart.

Austrian scientist, philosopher and artist, Rudolf Steiner (February 1861 – 30 March, 1925) said in a talk given in 1914 that human beings constantly interact with darker energies. However, there is a space within the heart that cannot be reached by such influences and it is from here that balance is maintained.

When we connect to this sacred place with conscious intent, no artificial structure can connect us to an inharmonic frequency, nor can we be disconnected from our Divine beingness.

IT IS INDEED AN ART TO LISTEN TO THE HEART.

AUTHOR'S MUSINGS

"The web of life is broken and like spiders who courageously set about a new weaving, we too are at that stage in the evolutionary process. Our web is beyond repair and, yet, we have a knowing, deep within that a new day is on the horizon, a new web is being woven and we are the weavers."

Broken threads of a broken web have bit by bit been pulled and an unravelling is creating chaos and confusion. Brave warriors cut away the bits of tangled, weakened threads using swords of light that only those coming from a place of love and integrity know how to wield. The Giant's 'merrymen' use bullying tactics such as the decimation of food supplies and the manipulation of the weather, but those stories are not mine to tell. However, they will be told and the underbelly of a dark agenda will be lanced like an infected tooth. Shadows that creep into our dreams and are the stuff of nightmares will be gone.

Like a Trojan horse, the dark has infiltrated every aspect of society over a long time and it will take time to 'pull out the weeds' so to speak, and re-create the Garden of Eden.

I thought to finish on 'words of wisdom' however, there are none. I could only remain within the heart space where humanity's tears are collectively felt at this time. We truly are all connected through the spirit of Grace and it is here that the trauma of Earth's journey through the dark lands will be released. It is through the Grace of the Creator, whatever you perceive the Creator to be, that the broken can be healed.

However, we too are a spark of that greatness and we too have been a part of this awakening and that is a truth worth rejoicing. Everyone has a part to play and a gift to give. Whether awake or asleep, just being here at this time and bringing a spark of light to the dark is perhaps more courageous than we can imagine. Those who chose to remain 'asleep' or 'sat on the fence' have played a part, perhaps, in prompting others to find their heroic nature.

The dark side has played a part by creating experiences that can enrich and fortify the soul. Just when it seemed like there were no more heroic journeys to embark on, we found ourselves witness to the darkest and the brightest time on Planet Earth. The brightest is in the knowing that we have an opportunity to address the darkness and embrace a new and enlightened way of living.

In the mean-time enjoy life, hug, kiss, sing, dance and have fun, which is what the Giant and its 'merrymen' do not want.

And, in closing, I write these words:

Every hug creates a vortex through which love can enter

Every smile, a drop of hope

A kind word will lift the spirits of all who hear

A hand given in friendship is a gift

When a human sings, the whole of creation knows that all is in perfect order

It always was and always will be

Namaste

EPILOGUE

THE YEAR 2023

The year 2023 was welcomed by watching from my son's balcony the fireworks that many travel long distances to see. However, the magic I had experienced throughout my life when witnessing such a spectacle, had dimmed.

The glass of champagne had lost its usual allure.

I believe I have been embroiled in personal battles with the dark however, nothing prepared me for the sudden and brutal change that happened in my own life towards the end of the year 2022.

One moment I was in great health leading an independent life and the next, I was savagely thrust into an abyss of helplessness and critical ill health and in a hospital fighting for my life. After three long weeks of nightmare, the diagnosis was metastatic breast cancer with no treatment options except for the hope of a new drug to contain and stop the march of the invading cancerous cells. I had become weak and defenceless and with a broken arm due to a fall, rendered helpless. The cancer I had successfully overcome in the year 2012 had returned with a vengeance.

I had a personal battle to contend with and this was my new reality. I was oblivious to the world situation and my world had shrunk to focus on my fight to survive.

The endless hospital procedures had taken their toll and I was taken to my youngest son's home to live, now totally dependent on another for my every need. I was blessed, someone cared so much that I was spared further hospitalisation and then an extended stay in a care situation. I was given a chance to regain my health and independent life and at the time of writing, I am taking baby steps towards this goal. Dr Henry Ealy, a world renowned expert in naturopathic medicine, commented that someone needs to run the marathon, or there is no hope. I was fortunate in that someone made the commitment to run the marathon and others stepped in to lighten the burden.

Like Sleeping Beauty, I closed my eyes whilst living in one reality and woke to a very different one. My health was now challenged and my peaceful hinterland home was no longer an option as a place of refuge. My precious cat was adopted by a neighbour and my 'possessions' were placed into storage. I embarked on another challenge, another adventure.

I believe that I am living proof of someone who can survive those treacherous times of being thrust into the arms of evil. You may ask, how it was possible to go from being critically ill with my life force floating in and out of this consciousness to making a slow and steady recovery to once again experience a cancer journey.

My 2012 cancer journey taught me that to regain health and wellbeing, I needed to become aware of how to navigate a minefield of situations such as heavy metal toxicity, harmful chemicals, microwaves, electromagnetic frequencies and emotional, psychological and spiritual toxicity. Since that time, I have endeavoured to bring healing modalities into my everyday living. These include eating organically grown food, sourcing clean spring water, grounding, spending time in nature, gentle yoga, prayer and meditation.

I believe the critical message to give is that everything you do towards health and wellbeing is spiritual currency. If I had not been in a place of wellness when a dark force hurtled me to the ground (which is what this felt like at the time), then I would not have had the opportunity to regain strength and vitality. Friends who share my wellness lifestyle are saying, "Now we know why we live like we do and that is to ensure a greater chance of recovery in times of ill health."

That is a powerful message.

I am living proof of this way of thinking and believe I would not have survived if I had had no healthy reserves to draw upon.

A friend once said, "If no-one's there, you don't come back." This is so true. I came back because there was someone there for me and what I remember of those early days of my hospital journey was seeing my youngest son. He was always there as was my daughter-in-law, who supported me with healthy food and water. She was there to hold me when those dark wings came flapping. I also believe it was because my doctor popped in and out and from comments heard, I knew that he was fighting for my survival.

I had a wonderful team of practitioners waiting to take on the task of rebuilding and replenishing and I am growing strong in spirit because family and friends stepped forward to give support, love and healing.

These writings are focused on brave warriors speaking in the public domain, risking everything to ensure that humanity's soul survives this journey to seed future generations. However, every-day men, women and children also walk this path. When we are open to the lives of those around us, we see the spirit within and become a witness to the soul's heroic struggle to survive and flourish.

I spoke to a neighbour who spends time every day visiting her husband in a nursing home as he is needing care that she cannot give to him. She said that he believes he is fortunate as he is living to see his grandchildren. There are many gifts in our everyday living, however, not everyone has the eyes to see.

The markets where I shop have a system in place to support in the way of putting together produce for those unable to do so and, also to make it possible for these people to effortlessly receive this precious bounty. They say that this is what we do when we can. The stories are many and are told by everyday heroes. This is how we keep the spirit alive and nurture the soul.

I recently listened to someone speaking about an adventure he had with sea creatures while diving in the ocean. He said that these are the times essential for enriching our soul which he believed is shrivelling in today's world. A profound statement and one that bears more than a passing thought and a reminder to embrace those soul enriching experiences when they are encountered.

Humanity has compassion and warmth. The human heart has the ability to encompass and heal those in need. Humanity has the capability to create beauty and that space of love for all living creatures to be held in a place of peace. Artificial intelligence, a force with intent to shrivel the human soul and cut away the human ability to bring spirit into the physical realm, does not possess these qualities. Acts of love ensure that the human spirit will survive these dark times and are the foundations upon which our new world is being built.

When we live in generosity of spirit, we are the heroes.

When the time came for me to delve once again into the evolving Covid story, I was amazed to find that there was an appearance of little change. However, everything had changed and some people were slowly but surely waking up and rubbing their eyes. Many pretended that we had gone back to the 'old' normal and others joined the ranks of those fighting for freedom.

I awoke to a world divided.

However, truth was slowly coming to light and brave warriors from all walks of life were stepping forward with bits of the puzzle. Voices from those carrying out diligent research into factual documentation were being heard despite the censorship imposed on all levels of communication.

Karen Kingston, a pharmaceutical and medical device business analyst, published *The Kingston Report*, showing that what we were told was a 'safe and effective' vaccine and the only solution to the 'pandemic', was not true.

On 30 January, 2023 Lieutenant General Igor Kirillov, Chief of the Russian Military Nuclear Biological and Chemical Protection Troops, gave a public briefing on information acquired on military biological programmes. Implicated are the US military, biopharmaceutical companies, universities, world health organisations, governments worldwide and private investors. He revealed that the Ukraine bio-laboratories have been creating highly infectious agents to target Russia and the world civilians and confirmed that mRNA injections are bioweapons. Their findings, he said, support Karen Kingston's analysis work on exposing Pfizer.

Alison Ryan in an exclusive report for *Cairns News* said that in October 2022, Russia had presented to the United Nations Security Council volumes of evidence collected when dismantling the Ukrainian and the United States owned and operated bio-laboratories situated along the Ukrainian border.

Russia acted with transparency while engaging the proper diplomatic channels to present this evidence and in doing so, revealed a possible violation of the Biological Weapons Convention (BWC). The BWC prohibits the development, production, acquisition, transfer, stockpiling and use of biological and toxic weapons.

Former United States Congresswoman, Tulsi Gabbard had reported in March 2022 that there are twenty-five to thirty active bio-laboratories in the Ukraine and approximately three hundred United States' funded bio-laboratories around the world. She called for these to be shut down and the deadly pathogens to be destroyed.

When future historians ask, "What were they thinking?" the voice of the people will echo through time saying, "We did not know."

Sasha Latypova worked for Pfizer for over 20 years. In later years her company worked on clinical trials for pharmaceutical companies. In 2020 when realising that the Covid story did not ring true, her investigations led to the realisation that this was a pre-planned global military campaign.

Ms Latypova combined her research with the legal framework of Katherine Watt, a paralegal and writer, who had investigated how the government was able to carry out this psychological campaign, trigger an emergency based on nothing and call a bioweapon a vaccine. A deep dive into the irregularities in documents threw light on how the weaponisation of health care became a reality for the people of the world and how the militarisation of health care placed power and control into the hands of the Giant and its 'merrymen'.

Sasha Latypova's interview with Robert F Kennedy Jr on Children's Health Defense streamed on 16 March, 2023 gives a powerful insight into this story. When asked about her exquisite painting, Daniel in the Lions' Den (one of many in her art portfolio), she said the message the painting told her was that God's design is perfect, absolutely perfect. You cannot improve on the truth and you cannot improve on the human body or the cells or the DNA. And, if you understand this, then you know there's nothing to be afraid of.

To hear her speak those words brought calm to my soul.

The time of Covid lifted the veil on another piece of the story. Nanotechnology, Karen Kingston said in 2023, "Is an unregulated 'dual-use' industry with military weapons and consumer applications that has been causing mild-to-severe cognitive dysfunctions, infertility, cardiovascular diseases, cancers and death for decades." Nanotechnology is widely used and can be found in electronics and smart devices, medical products, food, dietary supplements, cosmetics, water sanitisation and tobacco products. Ms Kingston wrote, "Industry experts are well-aware that the use of engineered nanoparticle technologies is rampant, harming biological life forms and our planet at an accelerated rate."

A former Fema employee specialising in nanotechnology and synthetic biology, Celeste Solum is releasing her research to bring understanding to the unfolding story and to expose the Giant's plan to replace all forms of biological life with synthetic biology. Her work is researched from government documents, medical journals and other credible sources of information. Celeste Solum told Maria Zeee (2023) that the 'new' humans began to come forward from the Covid-19 vaccinated.

Ensuring this information is reaching as many receptive ears as possible has been made possible by 'alternative news' journalists who give the warriors and whistleblowers a platform from which to speak.

Australia's Maria Zeee from *Zeee Media* has interviewed those from around the world who have an important story to tell and gives regular analysis of the documentation she has researched. She sent out a call to those with organisation skills to join in the venture to unite the people.

We must remember that anyone who speaks against the government narrative is risking the wrath of the Jackboots.

Ricardo Delgado, Jose Luis Sevillano (La Quinta Columna), Robert Young, Karen Kingston, Mik Anderson, David Nixon, Hope Feagin and Tivon Rivers, Mat Taylor and Ana Maria Mihalcea are voices to be heard on *The Intra-Body Nano Network Compilation* of September 2023. The presentation gives insight into the technology that has been deployed on the population of the world. Following are extracts:

> Documents such as The Operation Warp Speed Contract, the vaccine patents and the Pfizer documents they wanted to hide for seventy-five years have revealed that the Covid-19 jabs are technology and not biological.

> The patent titled, Vaccines Technology which is a utility patent for the Covid-19 jabs, lists components of the vaccine as agents of biowarfare. This technology then uses the cells of the body to make new lifeforms that are half natural and half unnatural, are self-assembling and fully programmable from the outside.

> Conductive hydrogels found in vaccines, masks and PCR swabs contain nanotech that can lock onto the DNA and can then be controlled by 5G sensors. It says, "Conductive hydrogels allow for tracking, tracing and biological and mental control of human beings."

"This technology will literally take away your body's sovereign rights," said Dr Robert Young.

Metals play an important part in the creation of the artificial organisms and are showered on us from many sources including geoengineering, through the food and water supplies, the vaccinations and the nasal swabs used for Covid-19 testing. A study by Aparicio-Alonso et al, released in September 2023, showed that nasal swabs contain titanium, zirconium, the metalloid silicon, aluminium, gallium, sulphur and fluorine. These can have a detrimental effect on the human body and migrate via the lymphatic system to the brain. The conclusion stated that the amount was close to reported toxicological thresholds for inhalation routes.

Ana Maria Mihalcea, board certified in internal medicine and who holds a PhD in pathology, has confirmed that she and her colleagues from around the world found metals and filament structures shown to self-assemble and to be receptive to electromagnetic frequencies in the Covid-19 jabs. This toxicity was found in the blood of the vaccinated and the unvaccinated and the 'shedding' or transmission of nanotechnology and synthetic biology is a question many are asking.

Dr Mihalcea asked, "What has happened to our blood?"

Mum wrote, "Love is in the blood."

I believe Mum was right, Spirit flows into every cell in our body via the blood. With the Giant's agenda coming to light to disconnect Life on Earth from Spirit, could this be what we are looking at when live blood analysis, as shown by Dr Mihalcea and others, reveals deformation of cell membranes instead of round living cells of light?

Angelo Drudo (2009) reminds us that the blood is the messenger transporting nutrients, qi and higher qualities. He wrote, "When blood production and circulation become weak, then it is not only our bodies that suffer, but our consciousness as well, leaving us feeling dull, unclear and in the most severe cases, depressed. Happily though, the reverse is true: when we increase blood circulation and production and tonify its quality, we can dramatically lift our spirits, increase our intellectual and creative capabilities and magnify our sense of existential wellbeing."

What Rudolf Steiner called the etheric or Life body is a fine subtle sheath (also a part of what is now known as the body's biofield) surrounding and intertwining throughout the physical body and relies on the blood to unify the process of health and wellbeing. When the blood is no longer strong, pure and free flowing, this process is diminished as is access to the 'bridge' that connects to higher sheaths that encase our soul.

However, I believe that higher vibrational states such as love, joy and peace can assist to counteract evil intent and maybe, it will be humanity's journey through the dark lands that will awaken us to its true potential.

We are the ones we have been waiting for and the ones talked about in the prophecies and we will be the ones talked about in the future history of mankind.

The David and Goliath story is a powerful blueprint and because of this, we 'know' that we can be victorious over an agenda to corrupt and enslave. We must come to understand that to act from a place of compassion and not hatred or revenge is important as there are different levels of awareness underpinning our present-day society.

The first are those who are enjoying the fruit of their effluent lifestyles as a reward for loyalty to the Giant. Many in this category which has shades of grey, are perhaps showing characteristics of a human who is very intelligent but has no affinity to the Spirit. This is a black and white world in which there is little warmth.

The second are those who live in fear. "Your head on a platter, or worse!" The shadow of their oppressor follows their every move, thought and deed. Or, so they believe. Fear for your life or of those you love is a powerful weapon. However, many are doing the best they can to protect self and families and this may involve becoming what is known as 'controlled opposition' and again, there are many shades of grey. A tactic the Giant appears to be very skilled at is to have a controlling hand in both sides of the story. Also, throwing doubt on another's integrity to cause separation, dissolution and chaos is another ploy frequently used.

The third category are those who are blissfully asleep. The indoctrination as they moved through the corridors of learning was so powerful that the spell cast over their lives is difficult to break. There are many contributing factors such as the programming from family, society and the media – injections given from birth, the poisoning of water with substances such as fluoride, food that is devoid of Life, light and nutrients and that contains dangerous chemicals such as glyphosate – the air we breathe containing toxic substances due in part to the chemtrail agenda. The list goes on and includes electromagnetic frequencies that are not in alignment with our frequency.

We are coming to understand that these frequencies are major players in creating imbalance in our physical, emotional and mental bodies.

And, then we have the few who have put on their spiritual armour and taken up the sword of truth. Some have been in the 'fight' for a long time and have laid a solid foundation to support the growing number of warriors joining their ranks.

However, we do not know the journey of soul. We do not know another person's destiny. We can only follow our own inner guidance and show up in our lives each-and-every day. Many years ago, I took my mum to see the musical theatre production of *The Lion King*. She was at that time using a walking stick for support following the trauma of a broken hip due to a fall. The theatre was beautiful, old and ornate with a winding marble staircase and our seats for the performance were at the top of that staircase.

For mum, this would have been a nightmare to navigate. There was no lift in the building and her choices were to retreat or to tackle those stairs, which she valiantly began to do with not a whimper or a grimace. The theatre was packed with school children and suddenly, a young man appeared, scooped her into his arms and valiantly carried her to the top of those stairs. He was a teacher and that day, showed those young children what it means to be the hero in your own life.

There are times in our lives when we have an opportunity to carry out an act of heroism. That simple act may make all the difference to the life of another and give them the opportunity to walk again, laugh again, love again and experience Life again. Those who are jab injured, those mourning the loss of loved-ones, businesses, homes and life-style, those suffering mental health issues, to name but a few casualties due to the Covid era may need carrying for a time.

Every breath is an opportunity.

Despite contracts between governments, the pharmaceutical companies and the defence industry that do not allow independent researchers the freedom to examine the vials containing the

Covid-19 jab or to carry out independent research, questions are now being asked.

Dr Ana Maria Mihalcea said the Covid-19 bioweapon is a very advanced artificial intelligence nanotechnology that can connect us to the internet of things. This technology is bombarding us from everywhere including the biosphere. Clifford E Carnicom, Len Ber MD, Dr Shimon Yanowitz an independent researcher from Israel, Electrical Engineer Matt Taylor and others from around the world support her findings, including Australian physician, Dr David Nixon.

Dr Nixon was one of the first to reveal nanotechnology that did not belong in dental anaesthetics and medications, leading to the ongoing exploration of other substances. He was one of the first to film real time footage of assembling robotic arms that guide the nanotechnology found in the Covid vials.

When being interviewed by Maria Zeee (2022) he said, "We need to stop all vaccinations, I mean all vaccinations, right now until we understand what is going on here."

However, scientist Clifford Carnicom has for twenty-five years been studying the geoengineering of our skies and documenting the nano material such as heavy metals and strange filaments that have been aerial sprayed. He studied filaments sprayed that could not be identified and caused lesions and fibres to grow out of human bodies, called Morgellons. When joining forces with Dr Ana Maria Mihalcea, it was discovered that these filaments are the same as the hydrogels, the metals and the nanotechnology found in the Covid-19 jab.

Drs Morell, Cowan and Kaufman asked in the *Statement of Virus Isolation* the question, "What is going into those injectable devices erroneously called 'vaccines' and what is their purpose?"

Dr Mihalcea's research into the childhood 'vaccines' showing the Human Papillomavirus vaccine (HPV) given to nine-to-twelve-year old children contains nanobots, self-assembly hydrogel and polymer mesh development. She said, "Bottom line, all vaccines have self-assembly nanoparticles in them."

When finding nanobots, quantum dots and self-assembly hydrogel in the MMR – measles, mumps, rubella and varicella vaccine – Dr

Mihalcea wrote, "If you have a soul left, you cannot poison one more child with this. Ever again. Parents who love their children, you cannot buy into this vaccine propaganda again. NOBODY can justify this material into babies."

Dr David Nixon told Maria Zeee (2022), "We need to stop 4G, 5G and wireless – we need to stop the things we know that are causing these things to grow and that definitely is EMF."

Dr Reiner Fuellmich (ICIC.LAW) interviewed Barrie Trower, an expert in the field of microwave radiation and frequencies, a former intelligence officer with M15 and M16, a scientist and a university lecturer. Using documentation, Barrie Trower revealed that these frequencies have been used in human experimentation such as mind control, geoengineering, weather manipulation and crowd control since the 1930's. He spoke of the detrimental effects on the health and wellbeing of all creatures on Earth. When hearing the long list of symptoms caused by these frequencies, Dr Fuellmich commented that Covid-19 symptoms are identical and the true cause could be microwave radiation.

Many are asking the same question.

A 2020 Spanish study was the first to demonstrate a clear relationship between the rates of coronavirus infections and 5G antenna location. Translated from the Spanish by Claire Edwards, the author, Dr Bartomeu Payeras I Cifre1 is a biologist, specialising in microbiology, who works at the University of Barcelona (Radiation Dangers).

Angela Tsiang and Magda Havas published a study in 2021 showing that where 5G technology was active, the highest case severity and death rate from Covid in the United States had occurred.

Naima Feagin (Hope) and Tivon Rivers researched and released information on the Wireless Body Area Network (WBAN), a system that has been put into place to access the human body to receive and transmit data. In an interview with Maria Zeee (2023) they said, "Humans are being bio-hacked through the Wireless Body Area Network, which is an AI driven technology that has been covertly erected round our modern society over the past several decades. It uses our living human bodies to operate.

"The system was recently upgraded through Covid and is going full steam ahead to implementing the UN 'Age of Global Enlightenment' which is, in-reality, Technocratic Totalitarianism." They believe that it is this technology that is causing the diseases we have been seeing increasing for a long time and said, "When you start to attack the body with these frequencies, the result is all these illnesses." And, suggest that looking at the biofield to correct the energy imbalances may be a key to treating illness.

The human biofield (aura) now proven to exist by modern-day science has been well documented and taught in many cultures from knowledge handed down from ancient texts such as the Hindu *Vedas*. These scriptures were-considered-to-be so sacred that they could not be written but were passed on from teacher to disciple by word of mouth and only brought together in a written form at around 3,100 BC. Although this knowledge has been suppressed in recent times, the whispering of those ancient voices can still be heard for those with the ears to hear.

Ancient whisperings talk of our body as being a highly refined system and when in tune can play a song that is unique to us, a song that speaks of the Divine within. Every cell in our body would then become a powerhouse of energy capable of overcoming frequencies that are not melodic to our vibration. An imbalance from a toxic environment, discordant electromagnetic frequencies and our belief that this is not possible are contributing factors to preventing this from happening.

The human cell contains a seed of Divinity, a touch of the Creator or God. However, when fused with technology, that seed can never open and blossom. Our cells would then become part of a machine, capable of receiving and transmitting the programming of the AI world. They would have lost the ability to become living breathing Divine Love.

Nevertheless, pieces of the puzzle are slowly falling into place with a picture beginning to form of the end goal the Giant and its 'merrymen' believe they will achieve. The web silently woven over a long period of time has allowed this predator, like a thief in the night, to unleash a dark agenda in-an-attempt to capture the Spirit of Creation.

The Spirit of Creation is Life and can never not be. However, we can create a world of beauty or a world of shadows.

The Covid-19 jab, said to be a key part in moving the Giant's agenda forward, has had devastating effects. Stories from around the world reveal the cold eye that governments, health authorities and the media portray to excess death rate reports for the years 2021 – 2022 and continuing. They say, "Nothing to see here." They urge, "Take another safe and effective jab." Excess deaths means that there is an unexplained rise in mortality since the jab was introduced in January 2021 but was not the case in 2020 when the 'virus' was said to be most virulent. The excess death data is soaring in lockstep world-wide.

Mike Capuzzo (2023) reported on the newly released forty-five page report based on government and insurance industry data showing that young people aged 15-44 years of age in the United Kingdom are dying from rapidly metastasising and terminal cancers at an unprecedented rate since the mass Covid-19 vaccination began. The report by Ed Dowd is a follow-on from his previously published, *UK – Death and Disability Trends for Cardiovascular Diseases, Ages 15-44* and the *UK – Death Trends for the Cardiovascular System. Ages 15-44, Analysis of Individual Causes*.

In March 2023, Senator Ralph Babet put forward two motions that excessive deaths from the Australian Bureau of Statistics for the years 2021 and 2022 be acknowledged and investigated. Although the motions were defeated, the Australian Medical Professionals Society (AMPS – operating as an alternative to the Australian Medical Association) took the banner and are enquiring into Australia's excess mortality.

They have released a book, *Too Many Dead – An Inquiry Into Australia's Excess Mortality*. They said, "The number of dying Australians constitutes an unfolding catastrophe and we owe it to all those dead Australians and their grieving families and friends to investigate what is killing at such an alarming rate. Failure to seek answers is negligent and beyond disrespectful."

On 20 October, 2023 Andrew Bridgen, MP for North West Leicestershire, United Kingdom, gave a speech on excess deaths to a full cheering public gallery. Sadly, the chamber where his fellow members of parliament sat was almost empty and few in this group heard his words that excess deaths are striking down people in the prime of life but no-one seems to care (Elijah, 2023).

In New Zealand, Barry Young, a statistician and a data-base administrator, released government data showing evidence of excess deaths in his country. When comparing the mortality from different injection sites around the country, a story with horrifying implications was revealed. He explained to lawyer and journalist, Liz Gunn (FreeNZ, 2023), "Statistics are showing that something is wrong and it is concentrated in the South Island with mortality rates far in excess of what is normal." And, "This is not a natural event, this is man-made."

The New Zealand Jackboots had enforced strict vaccine mandates. However, when Barry Young's data was presented to the health authorities and government officials, it was brutally dismissed.

Barry Young said, "This data is a river of tears and I feel the pain."

In an interview with Liz Gunn, his response when she said that what he was offering to the people of New Zealand and the world is heroic, he replied that the heroes are the guys who stood at the gate in the freedom march, who were brave enough to push back. He said, "The women who took the rubber bullets from the police who were meant to protect and serve us, the ones who stood firm and lost their jobs because they were told to get a procedure they did not want. They were brave enough to say, "No". They are the heroes. I am not a hero." However, could Barry Young's bravery in releasing this information to the world be a catalyst in unravelling the Giant's web?

Following this interview, Barry Young received a visit from the New Zealand Jackboots, his home was surrounded for hours before being raided and he was taken into custody. It was reported that he received a standing ovation from a full public gallery on his first bail hearing. He shouted, "Freedom" to the gallery. Another whistleblower supporting Barry Young's data was also subjected to the Jackboots' tyranny.

Liz Gunn appealed to the world, "You either stand by these whistleblowers or you are going to see this sort of tyranny come to your door, your home in future years and if not you, the doors of your children. We will all be prisoners in future years if the world does not stand by, and with, these whistleblowers (Exposing the Darkness Newsletter, 2023)."

Excessive deaths worldwide are triggering serious questions and calls for a radical rethink of Covid vaccinations.

In January, 2024, a paper was published by Mead M, Seneff S, Wolfinger R, et al to look at the aftermath of the Covid-19 mRNA vaccines. This included the increase in Serious Adverse Events (SAE) in the vaccinated, in the Pfizer trials and following the Emergency Use Authorisation (EUA), as well as inadequate safety and toxicological testing. The SAE's included death, cancer, cardiac events and various autoimmune, haematological, reproductive and neurological disorders.

It was reported that there was no excess mortality attributed to Covid-19, however, from March 2021 to February 2022, there were approximately 61,000 excess deaths among Americans under the age of 40. This was equivalent to all the servicemen from the United States of America who lost their lives during the Vietnam War (Brighthope, 2024).

The health decline on a worldwide scale can no longer be ignored and questions that should have been asked are now on the table.

"Australia has the best health care in the world," I was told when I was recently hospitalised. However, Dr Phillip Altman in his Substack wrote, "When push comes to shove, we now need to realise that our current Government has no real interest in the health of Australians – all the talk of ensuring Australians are safe and providing the best health care possible is a joke."

Practitioners worldwide risk everything to bring to the public arena this awareness that is a worldwide situation. Dr Rashid Buttar was a formidable warrior who left our Earthly realm on 18 June, 2023. He had openly and fiercely opposed the Giant's agenda, had been in the 'fight' for a long time and revealed before his passing that he believed he had been intentionally poisoned. When speaking of this experience to Dr Bryan Ardis in 2023, he said that he had received a message to mankind from the Creator and that was to exercise Freewill – God is in control and everything else will fall by the wayside.

The Law governing creation says, 'Do No Harm' and if violated will have terrible consequences.

It is time for humanity to come together to fight for the freedom that is the birthright of every living being on Earth. Division is a tool successfully used by the Giant and its 'merrymen' to create chaos and confusion. Dr Ana Maria Mihalcea in her Substack wrote of the analogy between the book (and the movie) called, *The Lord of the Rings* and the situation we are in today. In this epic writing, many united to face the existential threat, to be taken over by absolute evil and perish. They did not necessarily like each other but put their differences aside to unite to tackle a formidable foe. She says that the bottom line of the movie is, "We are under siege - we unite and fight or perish."

During the years 2020 to 2022, the planet was brutally thrown into darkness.

The Giant, having captured every aspect of the peoples' societies, openly proceeded to take away the right to free speech. Only the narrative as written by the tyrant would be permitted and many were deplatformed from speaking in the public square. Through the official channels of information and communication, a new 'reality' was emerging. Those who saw a different picture, were silenced and persecuted.

History was being rewritten.

The Jackboot was firmly placed on the face of those who were not obedient.

The oppressive darkness suppressed a growing homeless, poverty-stricken portion of the population.

The music stopped.

However, those lights that refused to be extinguished began to glow with even more intensity attracting other lights to blink and glow. Voices were heard to say, "No, We Will Not Comply." The human spirit, alive and well as we moved through the year 2023.

In Australia, people were making, drawing and sewing daisies.

Daisies for Dazelle, a community-based fundraiser was founded to support sixteen-year-old Dazelle Peters who needed a double lung transplant. Australia's St Vincent's Hospital situated in Sydney, refused to put her on the transplant list unless she took four Covid-19 jabs, which would have taken nine months to administer. Dazelle's story began when she received a diagnosis of leukaemia at the age of thirteen. However, the treatment she received led to a deterioration of her lungs and those magical years of moving from childhood to becoming a teenager became a battleground for survival. Every daisy is a drop of love for Dazelle, to give support to the family and to raise awareness of medical discrimination.

Daisies for Dazelle united with the Heart for Vicki fundraiser. Vicki, a mother of two children was being denied the opportunity to receive a life-saving heart transplant due to her vaccination status. The Daisies for Dazelle and the Heart for Vicki fundraisers brought people together through children's activities, singing, dancing, hugging, laughing and being human.

Michael Gray Griffith, Australia's *Cafe Locked Out*, tells the story of Dazelle's courage and her family who ran the marathon every day to give a loved one the hope that was taken away by uncaring medical professionals. And, Hope is a powerful medicine.

Two teenage children whom I know refused to take the Covid-19 jab. Their parents supported their decision despite having themselves succumbed to forced injections to keep their jobs. Born of an Australian parent and a Japanese parent, these children had spent their life in Japan up until this time when coming to Australia.

Coping with the challenges of settling into a culture that was foreign to them, with high school education and the fact that English was not their first language, they were faced with ridicule from friends and family. Family members insisted they were not to be invited to the Christmas gathering. However, loving, supportive and insightful parents gave these children a firm platform on which to stand and be like bamboo, strong, resilient and able to gently flow with the dark winds that may come.

Children relentlessly facing the challenges of today and the parents who expand their hearts to encompass and support them are heroes. And, from the young to the elderly, from all walks of life, creed and culture, warriors are emerging to fight for the human spirit to prevail.

Café Locked Out say that the Freedom Movement has instilled enough doubt within the minds of the people that many are now refusing Covid boosters. It said, "Simultaneously globally, the leper scientists and defiant doctors working together, all unfunded, have won the science battle. Now it is time for another demographic to rise and win the cultural war. The artists." Voices that were locked out of society responded to the platform offered here. The music began to play songs about the wounding, the history of this period-of-time and of hope for a renewed soul connection.

Few realise that musicians too have been captured by the Giant whose tentacles have squeezed the soul and heart out of creativity. Music that can lift the vibration to that of love, peace and joy has been replaced by a deadened drone-like beat. It can be heard everywhere and when combined with flashing lights can have a serious negative effect on the physical, mental and emotional aspects of our being.

In contrast, beautiful works of art, music, heartfelt writings and inspirational architecture can assist to raise consciousness and can be inspirational and timeless. When we lift our voices in song, all boundaries fall away and we become one voice, one united humanity.

Sasha Latypova said, "Whatever the globalists don't like, do more of it and harder."

And, the globalists do not like it when humans put their differences aside, come together in love and bring compassion, beauty, laughter and joy into the world. These are the acts that open a gateway to soul. When our soul is enriched and sings its' unique vibrational note that is true for each-and-every being, this is our gift to the world as when that unique note unites with others on the same vibration, an orchestra of souls can play a musical composition that will lift the vibration of the whole universe. This is what can happen when we put our differences aside and come together with one goal, such as the fight for freedom for the beings of Earth and beyond.

A River of Tears

My soul will find a way
Hold my hand, listen to what I have to say
Hear my heart talk
Know it is not your path to walk
Listen to what I have to say
For my soul will find a way
Catch my tears
Hear my fears
All I need is for you to listen
See the tears glisten
For my soul will find a way
Know that for one moment in a day
You were a witness to my pain
The voice of my inner blame
The egos ploy to divert my path to worldly ways
From the place where my inner child plays
Hold my hand, listen to what I have to say
At the end of the day
My soul will find a way

Robyn Robins, 2015

> *"Rest in Peace, the many souls taken. May our divided families heal. And for those suffering – gain the support and formal recognition that they truly deserve."*
> Selkie, 2023

My niece baked bread.

Later that day when we had gathered, she broke bread and this ritual was the foundation for a family gathering. We barbequed and ate in an atmosphere of appreciation and togetherness.

It had been years since I had seen my nephew and my heart cried when meeting his two boys. My youngest son and his children met for the first time, these family members. Bonding was immediate, the years of family gatherings had melded into an invisible pot that now overflowed with joy.

My nephew and his sons had been part of the family entourage that had only days before scattered my mum's ashes. The old crone's spirit had been laid to rest and today, I stepped into the role of the family crone. My niece, the mother and my granddaughter, the maiden, two faces of woman, completed the picture.

My son and his cousins had grown to be young men wearing the mantle of manhood through battles won in the University of Life. Their sons now tottered on the brink of initiation into this school under the watchful eyes of their fathers. There was no grandfather present however, the spirit of the elder male was alive and well in the minds and hearts of those present.

When the meal was complete, we walked onto the beach and I snuggled into the warm sand to watch the younger generations dive into the waves with revitalised strength, having now experienced the renewing of family bonds.

The elements of fire, earth, air and water cleansed and healed the wounds of the past years, the family spirit, alive and flourishing as we moved into the year 2024.

However, many families will be mourning members who will not celebrate the coming of a new year. It is important that these men, women and children are honoured and remembered by a collective community. The Forest of the Fallen started in 2021 by a woman called Selkie, a Tasmanian mother of three is a silent open vigil, a sea of faces with corresponding stories on bamboo sticks. Displayed around the country in public places such as parks and beaches, these memorials give us an opportunity to reflect and behold from a place of safety. A place from which to observe our collective woundings and acknowledge those who suffered. A space of heartfelt love where we can give gratitude to those departed souls.

David Kessler (2019) said, "We need a sense of community when we are mourning because we were not meant to be islands of grief. The reality is that we heal as a tribe. There is no greater gift you can give someone in grief than to ask them about their loved one, and then truly listen. When we see our sorrow in the eyes of another, we know our grief has meaning. We get a glimpse, maybe for the first time since the loss, that we will survive, and a future is possible."

When council workers take down the memorials, they say, "I am doing my job."

However, the Forest of the Fallen, like mushrooms, continues to pop up and each photo has a story to tell of a life lived. Story telling has always and always will be a means of passing down knowledge, wisdom and culture. The Giant's attempt to alleviate the telling of a story can never be successful.

Like those council workers who mindlessly follow a dark agenda, we too may take this path or listen to the heart's whispering that this is not the way. The heart is our compass and when we ignore its gentle promptings and go against our inner instincts, a dimming of our soul's light is the result.

Grieving will be an important part of our journey as humanity moves into a more enlightened time. Enriched forever by our soul memory of the knowledge and wisdom gained, Humanity's tears must flow to wash the dry arid landscape of death and decay to allow the seeding for the dawning of a new era. This is the legacy we gift the future generations and stems from that gifted to us by our ancestors, from those who fought for freedom and whose hearts kept the human spirit alive by the giving of love, hope and compassion.

My daughter who has been in the mental health system for a very long time said to me, "Mum, cry for me, I can't cry. Cry for me Mum." And, I did.

When another cannot cry, we cry for them. Silent prayers, "Cry for me" will be heard and tears like droplets of water will become a river of tears. Humanity will cry tears of pain, tears of grief, tears of healing and tears of joy. Artificial Intelligence does not have this ability, those carrying out the dark agenda have lost this ability.

We are beings of Divine Light, always have been and always will be and it is time to throw off the dark shackles of illusion, give gratitude for this opportunity and walk forward as one community. With societal structures breaking down, we have the opportunity to create a world of beauty. Or, we can allow a transhuman agenda to be the creator of the world our children and grandchildren will inherit.

In closing, I write from a deep inner knowing that the Human Spirit will triumph.

And, when the children of the future ask, "What did you do when the world went down in flames?" We will remember Jonathan Otto's words, "Love and God will prevail" and Karen Kingston's words, "Truth Wins".

And, we will look the children in the eye and we will have a story to tell.

PART 4
RELATED BOOKS, DOCUMENTARIES AND WEBSITES

THE LION SLEEPS NO MORE

SAYS DAVID ICKE

"This is the time for humanity to take responsibility for its world. To stop pointing the finger and saying, 'It's them'. No. It's us. It's always been us. It's always been us throughout known human history who have handed our power to the few. Which is why, throughout human history, the few have always controlled the many."
David Icke, September 17, 2022 London –
Worldwide Rally for Freedom

Patriot Streetfighter, Scott McKay said, "Get in the fight to stop the bad things happening to humanity and when you get into that fight, you will know what to do next. The Universe moves with people who are moving. The universe doesn't move with anybody standing still doing nothing. When people set themselves in motion on a conscious plane to do something good, protective or otherwise for the kids or humanity, the universe starts to line up forces, people, circumstances, money, whatever it is to change the planet. That is what causes a spiritual ignition point to take form and start to catalise us moving."
Otto – Disease In Reverse, 2023

Max Igan said, "Under no circumstances should you be afraid of your own power. Under no circumstances should you be afraid of death. Always be true to yourself. Always speak what you feel, say what you feel and be the best friend you can be. Face Infinity without flinching. Walk the path of the warrior."
The Launchpad Podcast, 17 July, 2023

"Vaccine hesitancy is a healthy state of mind. To be an anti-vaxxer or someone who questions vaccines, that's an intellectually healthy position to take. We should all have scepticism. The Covid-19 vaccines have led to a massive number of injuries, disabilities and deaths. We should all be shocked, outraged. We all should be anti-vaxxers at this time. We should all have extreme vaccine hesitancy."
Dr Peter McCullough, The Truth About Vaccines, Remedy, Episode 5, 2023

Dr Henry Ealy said, "We have all been 'damaged' by the insidious attacks from the dark side, however, do not become a victim. We have a choice whether trauma becomes hurt or healing, it is up to us — pain is inevitable but what we do with trauma is up to us. Choose to turn that pain into strength and incorporate tools to assist with the body to heal. Victimhood, is a prison that we can choose not to live in but instead we can choose to transform it into something strong even though it is hard. Surrendering to the pain is harder, giving up is harder."
Otto, New Hope Series, 2023

WEBSITES

"Hold the line people and never surrender"
(*HOLD THE LINE* is a Freedom Song written and performed by Kelly Newton-Wordsworth and dedicated to the Freedom Fighters of Western Australia)

ALUMINIUM RESEARCH GROUP

HTTPS://WWW.ALUMINIUMRESEARCHGROUP.COM

Dr Christopher Exley PhD, FRSB, renowned United Kingdom scientist had been researching the effects of aluminium on human health. This valuable work was undermined by tactics such as having research funding blocked and enforced disciplinary actions. The Giant's agenda did not include his decades of research becoming known by the public on the dangers of aluminium. This included published research to support the theory that aluminium is a human carcinogen. Nor did it include the knowledge that silicon rich mineral water has been shown to remove aluminium from the body. Dr Exley's book, *Imagine You Are an Aluminium Atom* gives further insight.

   The Aluminium Research Group are world leaders in this field and their work recognised internationally.

AUSTRALIAN VACCINATION-RISKS NETWORK INC

HTTPS://AVN.ORG.AU

The AVN was started in 1994 by a group of parents and health professionals who were concerned about the lack of scientifically-based information on the 'other side' of the vaccination issue. This website is packed with information on vaccinations, the Covid story and updates on pending court cases. However, it is the Vaxxed Bus travelling around the country to give those injured a voice that remains at the heart of this heroic endeavour.

Our stories will one day write an accurate account of history in regards to the vaccine era.

CAFÉ LOCKED OUT

HTTPS://CAFELOCKEDOUT.COM

Cafe Locked Out, Michael Gray Griffith and Florence the Freedom Bus for the past two years have been recording Australian voices for Australians everywhere – "We are trying to capture the history they are already trying to erase."

Supported by Dr Paul Oosterhuis who practised in anaesthesia and critical care medicine for over thirty-two years until becoming the first doctor in Australia to be suspended for questioning the official Covid narrative. And, he was the first doctor to become unsuspended due his courageous stance in taking the Medical Council of New South Wales to the Supreme Court. He said that he did this without the assistance of lawyers and, they dropped his suspension.

Dr Oosterhuis says, "We're Team Humanity, Team Fun, Team Truth."

This is a platform that has not only brought important information to the people but hope, love and hugs to the wounded heart of the Australian people.

Warriors with wings, I say.

CELLULAR PHONE TASK FORCE

HTTPS://WWW.CELLPHONETASKFORCE.ORG/ARTICLES/

HTTPS://RADIATIONEMERGENCY.ORG

President Arthur Firstenberg (scientist, environmentalist, journalist and author) founded the Cellular Phone Task Force in 1996. This website provides education to the public concerning electromagnetic pollution, is an advocacy for an electromagnetically cleaner environment and provides support for those disabled by radiation from wireless technology and other resources.

The Global Radiation Emergency is an international coalition of health-focused initiatives dedicated to restoring the health and vitality of the Earth. It says that Radiofrequency (RF) Radiation is presently the greatest cause of ecological destruction and human disease.

Humanitarian Arthur Firstenberg passed away on 25 February, 2025 from an undiagnosed illness.

He said, "The only thing we can really do for the Earth is to stop destroying it. Then the Earth will take care of itself. Instead of trying to fix the whole planet, let us attend to our own simple lives."

DOCTORS FOR COVID ETHICS

HTTPS://DOCTORS4COVIDETHICS.ORG

Established in 2021 it says: "We are doctors and scientists from 30 countries, seeking to uphold medical ethics, patient safety and human rights in response to Covid-19."

mRNA Vaccine Toxicity – this book is free to download from the website.

"Always question what so-called experts tell you."

"Solidarity demands you step forward and come out when you see something going wrong," said Professor Arne Burkhardt MD, who came out of retirement to investigate the injury and death caused by the Covid-19 vaccines. He passed away on 30 May, 2023 and it was his wish that his findings reach as many people as possible. Dr Burkhardt's presentations on the pathological evidence of mRNA vaccine damage can be seen on this website.

Dr Thomas Binder holds a doctorate in immunology and virology, specialising in internal medicine and cardiology. After speaking against the Covid narrative, he was diagnosed with 'Corona insanity' and spent time in a mental health institution. His message to the public: "This modified RNA genocide is the greatest medical crime in human history, a humanitarian disaster of unprecedented proportions." Powerful presentations given by Dr Binder can be found on this website.

DR DIETRICH KLINGHARDT MD, PHD

HTTPS://KLINGHARDTINSTITUTE.COM/

KLINGHARDTPROTOCOLS

Dr Klinghardt is the founder of the Klinghardt Academy (USA), the American Academy of Neural Therapy, Medical Director of the Institute of Neurobiology, and lead clinician at the Sophia Health Institute, located in Woodinville, Washington. He is also Founder and Chairman of the Institute for Neurobiology (Germany) and (Switzerland). The Klinghardt Academy (USA) provides teachings to the English-speaking world on biological interventions and Autonomic Response Testing assessment techniques. The institute is dedicated to true biological approaches to healing.

From the beginning of the Covid story, Dr Klinghardt has treated patients and taught practitioners worldwide his science-based, successful protocols. His weekly online podcasts with Daniela Deiosso have become a community of light not only giving valuable information but ongoing support.

Dr Daniela Deiosso said, "We hear you. Even the little things are important."

DR HENRY EALY ND, BCHN

HTTPS://WWW.ENERGETICHEALTHINSTITUTE.ORG

HTTPS://MY.ENERGETICHEALINGINSTITUTE.ORG/HEALING-FOR-THE-AGES

Dr Henry Ealy is a naturopathic doctor with over twenty years clinical experience. He has a BSc in mechanical engineering and certified in holistic nutrition. Dr Ealy is one of many doctors working to support the people and his wisdom alone gives a panacea to many.

Dr Ealy tells us that natural medicine starts with prayer, natural medicine starts with meditation, natural medicine starts with faith, belief that you are going to heal. Now you are in the realm of natural medicine. Natural medicine is sleep, sunlight, exercise, fasting, making sure your air is clean, your water is clean and your food is clean. Natural medicine has a whole hierarchy to go through before you go into supplementation. Natural medicine seeks to enact the innate mechanisms of the body for healing. Natural medicine does not completely dismiss the role of emotion or of spirit in the human process (Otto, Disease In Reverse, Q & A, 2023).

The Energetic Health Institution is a place to learn how to regain health and wellbeing with loving support. It is a place to gain holistic health qualifications and a place to join a community that is creating a space to heal.

DR MARTIN PALL'S LATEST COMPILATION OF EMF MEDICAL RESEARCH

HTTPS://WWW.RADIATIONRESEARCH.ORG/RESEARCGH/

Written and Compiled by Martin L Pall PhD, Professor Emeritus of Biochemistry and Basic Medical Sciences Washington State University.

Radiation Research is an independent body whose aim is to educate the public with the facts regarding electromagnetic frequencies and their effects on the environment and health.

ELECTROMAGNETICHEALTH.ORG

The US 1996 Telecommunications Act tied the hands of local governments, preventing them from resisting towers and antennas in their communities on health or environmental grounds - even when harm became clear. This power grab by the federal government, which facilitated the build out of the antenna infrastructure across America by the wireless telecommunications industry has been a travesty for human, animal and planetary health - it must be brought to light and reversed.

The voices of some of the Western World's leading scientists on electromagnetic frequency technology can be heard here.

FRANCES LEADER

HTTPS://FRANCESLEADER.SUBSTACK.COM

The word virus means poison in Latin. The genetic sequence we call SARS-Cov-2 is a synthetic poison designed by a computer - proven in December 2020 in email exchanges with UK MHRA (Medicines and Healthcare Products Regulatory Agency) who approved the Pfizer BioNTech vaccine. These email exchanges can be seen at: https://francesleader.substack.com/p/sarscov-2-mrns-is-synthetic.

Frances Leader's compiled evidence confirming the link between electromagnetic frequencies and the health of humanity and nature, collated between January 2020 - December 2021, can be seen at: https://francesleader.substack.com/p/all-my-substack-articles-on-emfc19.

GEOENGINEERING WATCH: EXPOSING THE CLIMATE ENGINEERING COVERUP

HTTPS://WWW.GEOENGINEERINGWATCH.ORG

Dane Wigington says, "The very essentials needed to sustain life on earth are being recklessly destroyed by these programs. This is not a topic that will begin to affect us in several years, but is now already causing massive animal and plant die off around the world, as well as human illness. The debate over whether geoengineering programs are going on is now a moot point. We have more than enough data to confirm it. We have actual footage showing tankers spraying. The materials showing up on the ground are exactly the same materials mentioned in the numerous geoengineering patents and documents. Visit our website for a list of these government patents and documents."

The Dimming – documentary regarding climate engineering operations.

Graphene Rain, Scientist Sounds Alarm – *a* must watch report.

GLOBAL HEALING

HTTPS://GLOBALHEALING.COM

The founder of Global Healing in 1998, Dr Edward F Group III, DC, NP, has been a leader in the field of alternative health for decades is an alum of Harvard Business School and MIT Sloan School of Management and an author.

Dr Group told Healing for the Ages Conference: "Ultimately the root cause of all symptoms, the root cause of all disease is a toxic internal and external environment. If you clean up your environment, you have the proper air purification systems, you have the proper water that you are consuming, you have the right type of supplementation programme, you are taking care of yourself, you are not in a state of stress, anxiety and fear, these are all the things that strengthen your biofield or aura.

HEALING FOR THE AGES

HTTPS://HEALINGFORTHEAGES.COM

Dr Bryan Ardis, Dr Henry Ealy, Dr Edward Group and Dr Jana Schmidt have been working together since the beginning of the Covid story. Healing for the Ages conferences are the result of their tireless endeavours to bring groundbreaking information and natural solutions to healing from the Covid bioweaponry imposed on humanity from many sources. They offer protocols for removing synthetic biology, graphene oxide, heavy metals and plastic based on peer-reviewed research and real-world clinical experience. They offer community, love and hope.

HOW BAD IS MY BATCH?

HTTPS://HOWBAD.INFO

HTTPS://HOWBADISMYBATCH.COM

A valuable resource for tracking batch codes and associated deaths, disabilities and injuries from Covid-19 jabs, based on the VAERS data. A wealth of related data analysis and batch variability data.

Craig Paardekooper was inspired by the high degree of variation between toxicity levels in batches causing deaths and disabilities to create this website. He continues to keep the information updated and with time, this work is revealing that there may be a variation in substances contained within the batches that are carefully monitored and labelled by scientists. It also appears that there is a higher death rate from the Pfizer and Moderna vaccines in the United States and a higher disability rate in other Western countries.

Team: Dr Mike Yeadon - ex-head of Pfizer Respiratory Research
Alexandra Latypova - biotech
Craig Paardekooper - researcher
Walter Wagner - lawyer
Dr Jessica Rose - statistician

ICAN (INFORMED CONSENT ACTION NETWORK)

WWW.ICANDECIDE.COM

WWW.THEHIGHWIRE.COM

Del Bigtree, a renowned public speaker who has worked with Robert F Kennedy Jr is the recipient of multiple awards for television shows such as *The Doctors*. His work contributed to bringing to the notice of the public the brave mothers and fathers of vaccine injured children who are fighting to stop Big Pharma's push to forcibly inject everyone with vaccines – a product the United States Supreme Court on the 22 February, 2011 Bruesewitz vs Wyeth, called 'unavoidably unsafe'(LLC 1312,S.Ct. 1068, 179). He is a producer of the documentary, *Vaxxed* and now hosts *The HighWire,* a digital health media platform.

As founder of ICAN (Informed Consent Action Network), Dell Bigtree, has brought together legal expertise, such as Aaron Siri (Lead Counsel, ICAN Legal Team) to fight many issues relating to vaccines and the Covid story. These include mandates and requests to governing agencies in the United States to produce evidence to support vaccine efficacy and safety. ICAN's latest 'win', at the time of writing, was to halt the Washington DC law allowing doctors to vaccinate children eleven years of age and older without parental knowledge or consent.

On 21 October, 2022 the CDC's vaccine advisory committee unanimously voted to add the Covid-19 vaccine to the CDC's routine childhood vaccination schedule. Immediately following the vote, Aaron Siri received a call from Del Bigtree, to say that ICAN would support a legal challenge to any state that imposed a Covid-19 vaccine mandate to attend school. On 20 December, 2021 ICAN's legal team stopped San Diego's Covid-19 vaccine school mandate. The Court's decision that this was illegal effectively made any local vaccine mandate, for any vaccine, illegal.

ICIC.LAW – INTERNATIONAL CRIMES INVESTIGATIVE COMMITTEE

HTTPS://ICIC.LAW/EN/

This website contains interviews from around the world and from the Grand Jury the Court of Public Opinion. These testify to the facts that many believe will in the near future become a foundation for bringing the Giant and its 'merrymen' to face justice for the crimes against humanity.

Dr Reiner Fuellmich began the journey with the Corona Investigative Committee in March 2020 that led to the Grand Jury the Court of Public Opinion in 2022. ICIC.LAW has continued this work and has reported that an international group of lawyers and scientists are now proposing to join with the Maori people of New Zealand to begin court proceedings. Dr Fuellmich explained in an interview with David Sorensen that the New Zealand Maori people have not lost or seeded their independence which was enshrined in their Declaration of Independence, written in 1835. They have independence and sovereignty. Trials can legally be held under this Lore, called Tikanga, to bring to justice the perpetrators of the well documented crimes against humanity. Men and women of Goodwill have given the knowledge that has laid a foundation upon which others can now stand to become a force to ensure that Justice, Truth and the Human Spirit prevail.

Constitution Watch reported that on 28 June, 2023 a Grand Jury drawn from the people of the United Tribes of New Zealand/Nu Tireni, heard the Prosecutor of Te Wakanga/Court of Justice present an outline of evidence. The unanimous decision of the Grand Jury was that the evidence substantiated the charges that were laid against four senior members of Parliament. None of the accused appeared in Court. A trial by Jury Hearing was heard on 27 August, 2023 with criminal charges given and sentences handed down.

In September, the Wakaminenga Maori Government (WMG) held a tribunal during which one hundred and eighteen Members of

Parliament were accused and found guilty of supporting and facilitating the actions of the four convicted. On 17 October, 2023 a statement was issued prohibiting the importation, sale and use of the mRNA BioNTech medical technology and all derivatives.

Although no extradition treaty exists between Germany and Mexico, in October 2023, Dr Fuellmich was unlawfully deported from Mexico to Germany to be held at the Rosdorf maximum security prison.

All motions for Dr Fuellmich's release on bail were rejected.

After nine months imprisonment and whilst Court proceedings are continuing, he sent an audio message to the people on 15 July, 2024. Dr Fuellmich said that many prison guards are shaking their heads in disbelief and claim that never before has an inmate charged with an alleged misdemeanour been held in preliminary custody for nine months – been put in chains and guarded by heavy armed police officers wearing bulletproof vests when being transported to prison and back – been isolated from the other inmates and told not to talk to anyone.

However, he said that he cannot be broken because of the worldwide support he is receiving and the memory of his Grandmother who told him over and over and over again:

"Reiner, you can do and achieve anything you like but you must never let yourself go."

Meaning: take care of your body, wear clean clothes and be someone of integrity. Do not disappoint those who trust you and keep your promises.

Dr Fuellmich said, "These are very simple ground rules but I have always found them easy to follow."

Dr Fuellmich is now shining a light into the dark prison system.

KNOW YOUR RIGHTS

HTTPS://WWW.KNOWYOURRIGHTSGROUP.COM.AU

A wealth of information for the Australian people to understand their 'rights' and how freedoms have been taken from them. The

Know Your Rights group is a community of like-minded people who are willing to share the knowledge they have gained over many years to educate and inform people of their rights in all areas of their lives.

"It is important to understand what you know and what you don't know."

MY CYCLE STORY: A RESEARCH STUDY

HTTPS://MYCYCLESTORY.COM

An independent research study collecting data around women's cycle changes in the Covid era when the conversation on social media prevented this from happening. Founder and President, Tiffany Parotto, together with a team of scientists, researchers, data experts and doctors aim to bring awareness of independent research to the scientific community and the wider public. They say, "The need to research these occurrences and give a voice to the women who were silenced was obvious."

MY FREE DOCTOR

HTTPS://WWW.MYFREEDOCTOR.COM

Dr Ben Marble is the founder of *MyFreeDoctor.com*, an online Covid treatment platform where he was the first to successfully treat people for free during the Covid era. It is the birthing of a parallel medical system to support patients and not profit – to support the unvaccinated who are being refused treatment. For this work, he was nominated for a Nobel Peace Prize.

NATIONAL VACCINE INFORMATION CENTER (NVIC)

HTTPS://WWW.NVIC.ORG

HTTPS://THEVACCINEREACTION.ORG

HTTPS://WWW.MEDALERTS.ORG/INDEX.PHP

NVIC has been dedicated to protecting health and informed consent rights since 1982.

"The only voice our children have until they are old enough to make life and death decisions for themselves is the voice that we, their parents who know and love them best, give to them." - Barbara Loe Fisher, Co-founder and President (NVIC).

THE KINGSTON REPORT - TRUTH WINS

HTTPS://KAREN KINGSTON.SUBSTACK.COM

Karen Kingston, a biotech analyst is the author of *The Kingston Report* that is an evidence-based analysis of Covid-19.

"If God's people remain silent, we will be enslaved. The truth can *not* prevail if we don't speak up. We are to put on the full Armour of God and the sword of truth." – Karen Kingston, Infowars, August 2021.

"Why would you think that it is a vaccine and not a bioweapon if it's producing a bioweapon in your body?" – Karen Kingston, 26 October, 2021.

THE WAR ROOM/DAILY CLOUT PFIZER DOCUMENTS ANALYSIS REPORTS

HTTPS://DAILYCLOUT.IO

War Room/Daily Clout Documents Analysis Volunteers' Report Book is available in paperback on documented information from primary source Pfizer documents, other key medical studies and literature relating to the mRNA Covid 'vaccine' for the period March to December 2022.

Pfizer was Court ordered to release documentation used to access the safety and efficiency of Covid-19 jabs. Doctors, lawyers, scientists, data analysts and others answered the call and as at 30 April, 2023 have published 64 reports revealing that due to the hidden knowledge of a long list of potential side effects, informed consent was not given.

TRUTH FOR HEALTH FOUNDATION

HTTPS://WWW.TRUTHFORHEALTH.ORG/MEDICAL-FREEDOM/

The fight for medical freedom continues to escalate every day and the medical and legal professionals at *Truth For Health* are working tirelessly and urgently to educate, advocate for, and help individuals across many fields - medicine, science, private and federal employees, military service members and their families. *Truth for Health* has created a vaccine treatment guide based on the work of Dr Elizabeth Lee Vliet, Chief Executive Officer of the foundation. It has created a vaccine injury reporting system to do the work government systems are not doing.

US FREEDOM FLYERS

HTTPS://USFREEDOMFLYERS.ORG

US Freedom flyers are standing up for the airline personnel who are damaged by the Covid vaccines and endeavouring to ensure that the airline service continues into the future.

"Stand with us to fight these overbearing communistic mandates set forth by President Biden and enforced by the companies we serve. Complying with these illegal mandates is a danger to not only our health, but freedom as we know it. Take a stand today and join our cause to fight back. We are raising capital to fight the Biden Administration and these totalitarian companies in a court of law."

The president, Josh Yoder, updated Dr Christiane Northrup on 11 September, 2023 saying that they have noticed about a sixty-six percent myocarditis rate increase largely in the vaccinated but also in the unvaccinated population. Vaccine passport language, he said, is already in the fine print of many airline ticketing. Tyranny is not something that goes away and this is why we need the entire public to stand behind us. If they come back with mandates, this needs to be shut down on day one.

He said, "Never underestimate your power as a human being, when you take a stand, you encourage someone else to take a stand and it grows by leaps and bounds."

VAXED VERSUS UNVAXED LITIGATION: RAY L FLORES II ESQ AND GREG GLASER (HEALTH FREEDOM RIGHTS ATTORNEYS)

HTTPS://INFORMEDCONSENTDEFENSE.ORG

In a federal complaint filed December 2020 in the US District Court of California, constitutional litigators Greg Glaser and Ray Flores presented results of a pilot study showing unvaccinated adults and children are healthier than their vaccinated counterparts. If successful then every American would have been exempt from mandatory vaccination. The five-thousand-page document showing that vaccines are destroying public health contain a wealth of information.

However, the Federal Court ignored evidence showing that unvaccinated Americans are over twelve hundred percent healthier than the vaccinated. This case is now closed.

See the video: *Do Vaccines Make Us Healthier?*

Explore the case documents.

VAXXED III - AUTHORISED TO KILL

HTTPS://VAXXED3.ORG

A Tommy Burrowes production for Children's Health Defense Films LLC.

Children's Health Defense embarked on a nine-month journey across America to interview people on Covid hospital protocols and the aftermath of taking the 'vaccines'. Death, serious injury, lies and heartache tell heart-retching stories.

A documentary for the people by the people.

WORLD COUNCIL FOR HEALTH

HTTPS://WORLDCOUNCILFORHEALTH/PRG

We are dedicated to safeguarding human rights and free will while empowering people to take control of their health and wellbeing.

The World Council for Health reported on the trial of Prof Sucharit Bhakdi in Germany on 23 May, 2023. When a 'not guilty' verdict was given, the crowd waiting outside the courtroom cheered.

The World Council for Health wrote:

Dear Prof Bhakdi …. Thank you for your strength, perseverance, love for the truth and language of compassion for life in all its forms. Using truth in combination with the language of our hearts is a better way forward. Truth will prevail. Together, let us be the Light that guides our destiny.

BOOKS/ DOCUMENTARIES

"I do not believe God punishes. He designed punishment for the devil and his angels but didn't design punishment for us. Our lack of wisdom creates destruction."
Dr Daniel Nuzam – Vaccine Secrets Reloaded, 2021

Books are one of my favourite things – books that you can pick up and feel and get a sense of where the author is coming from. My eldest son found an antiquated book shop when on a trip and sent a photo. It oozed the wisdom and knowledge that can only be found in the untidy piles of books seen to be scattering the floor area. Here could be found a legacy from the heart of many an author from past times to the present.

I was witness to the time when many book shops and authentic book distributors in Australia were closed. New, shiny book shops opened filled with books that told stories prompted by artificial intelligence. Outlets where local authors could be supported to promote their work almost disappeared.

However, story-telling is at the heart of the human experience and perhaps the Covid era has awakened the impulse to tell the stories from which history will be told.

BAILEY, MARK

BAILEY, SAM

The Final Pandemic: An Antidote To Medical Tyranny

While dismantling not only the Covid narrative but the idea of contagious pandemics, this book is designed for 'easy reading'. It explains how new diseases are created out of thin air and explores the narrative attributing the blame to animals and various groups of people. The book dives into the world of contagion, explaining how cases are created such as through the PCR and looks at the relentless marketing campaigns that distort reality. It delves into how vaccines - one of the greatest medical frauds of all time - are used to transfer wealth from the public to a small number of corporations and vested interests.

Forward by Professor Tim Noakes, world-renowned sports and nutrition physician from South Africa – The Noakes Foundation – questioning the science.

BREGGIN, PETER R

Dr Peter R Breggin has been called "The Conscience of Psychiatry" for his many decades of successful efforts to reform the mental health field. His scientific and educational work has provided the foundation for criticism of psychiatric drugs, ECT and the drugging of children, and leads the way in promoting more caring and effective therapies. He has testified in more than one hundred trials and hearings in the United States and Canada, often on clinical psychopharmacology, mass murder and the drug industry. He has seventy peer-reviewed publications and has written more than twenty books including:

Talking Back to Prozac (1994 with Ginger Breggin)

Medication Madness: The role of Psychiatric Drugs in Cases of Violence, Suicide and Crime (2008)

Psychiatric Drug withdrawal: Guide for Prescribers, Therapists, Patients and Their Families (2013)

Covid-19 and The Global Predators We Are The Pray (2022 with Ginger Breggin)

This book has introductions by three leading Covid-19 treating physicians: Peter A McCullough MD, MPH, Vladimir "Zev" Zelenko MD and Elizabeth Lee Vliet MD. Attorney Robert F Kennedy Jr, the author of *The Real Anthony Fauci*, has also endorsed the book as the single most comprehensive analysis of the coalition of global predators behind Covid-19.

During the Covid era, Dr Breggin and Ginger Breggin supported the people through radio shows and podcasts. They have been in the fight for humanity's freedom for a long time. We owe them gratitude for their endurance and courage.

BROGAN, KELLY

Own Your Self

The surprising path beyond depression, anxiety, and fatigue to reclaiming your authenticity, vitality and freedom.

A Mind of Your Own

The truth about depression and how women can heal their bodies to reclaim their lives.

A Time for Rain

A beautiful children's book (for all ages) about the importance of tears.

The Reclaimed Woman

A woman alive is the most powerful force on this planet.

Dr Brogan is a holistic psychiatrist who threw away her prescription pad to work with a root-cause resolution approach to psychiatric syndromes and symptoms.

She said, "When we can move beyond our fear of our symptoms and into curiosity, we find that all illnesses – without exception – is the body's wisdom playing out its own highly designed and incredible personal way."

CENTNER, DAVID (EXECUTIVE PRODUCER)

Producers:
Kennedy Jr, Robert F

Cost, Curtis
Jenkins, Kevin D
Muhammad, Tony
Medical Racism: The New Apartheid – From the Post-Civil War era and the Tuskegee Experiment to the present, this documentary explores experiments on the black community.

CHOSSUDOVSKY, MICHAEL

The Worldwide Corona Crisis, Global Coup de'Etat Against Humanity – PDF e-book
Michel Chossudovsky is an award-winning author, Professor of Economics (emeritus) at the University of Ottawa, Founder and Director of the Centre for Research on Globalization (CRG), Montreal and Editor of Global Research. He is the author of thirteen books.

There Never Was a 'New Corona Virus' There Never Was A Pandemic. He said, "This is among the most important articles I have ever written," and is available at Global Research.

And, "The unspoken truth is that the novel coronavirus has provided a pretext and a justification to powerful financial interests and corrupt politicians to precipitate the entire world into a spiral of mass unemployment, bankruptcy, extreme poverty and despair."

COWAN, THOMAS

Dr Cowan's many published books on medicine, nutrition, homeopathy, anthroposophical medicine and herbal medicine include:
Breaking the Spell – the scientific evidence for ending the Covid delusion
Human Heart, Cosmic Heart
Cancer and the New Biology of Water
The Four-Fold Path to Heal
Vaccines, Autoimmunity and the changing nature of Childhood Illness
Commonsense Childrearing: Unconventional Wisdom for a Nourished Childhood

Dr Cowan challenges conventional medicine and challenges us to explore holistic health.

COWAN, THOMAS

MORELL, SALLY FALLEN

The Contagion Myth
Why viruses (including 'coronavirus') are not the cause of disease. The question is asked if the cause is not viral, then perhaps it is a kind of pollution unique to the modern age – electromagnetic pollution and toxic living conditions.

DOWD, EDWARD

Cause Unknown, The epidemic of Sudden Deaths in 2021 and 2022
Research based on the death, disability and hospitalisation data from resources such as American life and health insurance companies. Edward Dowd tells us that this data is "alarming". For example, the excess death rate for working Americans 44 years old and younger was 179% during the period July – September, 2021. In July 2021 vaccines were mandated for public and private employment.
Foreword by Robert F Kennedy Jr. Afterword by Gavin De Becker.

ENGELBRECHT, TORSTEN

KOHNLEIN, CLAUS

BAILEY, SAMANTHA

SCOGLIO, STEFANO

Virus Mania
Corona/COVID-19, Measles, Swine Flu, Cervical Cancer, Avian flu, SARS, BSE, Hepatitis C, AIDS, Polio, Spanish Flu ... How the Medical Industry Continually Invents Epidemics, Making Billion-Dollar Profits At Our Expanse.

FARBER, CELIA

Serious Adverse Events: An Uncensored History of AIDS

Twenty years research gives a look at the 'other side' of the AIDS story. This extensive work also sheds light on the parallels between the AIDS epidemic and the present day Covid Plandemic.

FIELD, TOPHER

Battleground Melbourne

This is an important documentary, including interviews with freedom fighters and real-life footage of protests and police brutality.

A snapshot of the "Covid Era" with commentary by Topher Field, winner of the Australian Libertarian of the Year award in 2022, of the Australian Libertarian Activist in 2016 and author of *Good People Break Bad Laws*. He said, "I inspire people to have the courage to do what is right, even when their government is wrong."

FIRSTENBERG, ARTHUR

Microwaving Our Planet: The Environmental Impact of the Wireless Revolution

The Invisible Rainbow: A History of Electricity and Life

The history of electricity and its correlation to the rise in previously unknown diseases such as cancer, heart disease, diabetes and Alzheimers.

And it is late autumn in the life of the Earth. We must prevent winter from coming, for there will be no spring if it does. It is up to all of us.

The Earth and I

The Earth and I is the human story, from two million years ago to today. It is about the environmental crisis. It is about technology. It is about choices.

FISHER, DONNA

EMF: Silent Fields: The Growing Cancer Cluster Story

More Silent Fields: Cancer and the Dirty Electricity Plague
"The age of electricity, which has changed our lives dramatically, both industrially and personally, and allowed us to live virtual twenty-four-hour days has contributed to death and serious disease." Ms Fisher points to the parallel rise in the disease spectrum we are seeing today.
Dirty Electricity and Electromagnetic Radiation
Light that Heals: Energy Medicine Today & Beyond
Donna Fisher is an Australian warrior who has been in the 'fight' for many years. She is part of the Australasian contingent of the world EMF Protection Project.

HUMPHRIES, SUSAN

BYSTRIANYK, ROMAN

Dissolving Illusions: Disease, Vaccines, and the Forgotten History
A look at the overlooked facts that show that vaccines, antibiotics and other medical procedures are not necessarily the reason for decline in mortality of infectious diseases.
The Dissolving Illusions Companion
There are no worthwhile vaccines, not even smallpox or tetanus and certainly not the polio vaccine.
Dr Susan Humphries took the Road Less Travelled when witnessing the harmful effects of vaccines. From a renowned physician to leading a life of hardship and persecution, she continued to record valuable information that would otherwise have been lost to future generations.

ICKE, DAVID

David Icke has written and self-published over twenty books including:
Human Race Get Off Your Knees – The Lion Sleeps No More
The Biggest Secret
The Truth Shall Set You Free
Alice in Wonderland and the World Trade Center Disaster – Why the Official Story of 9/11 is a Monumental Lie

The David Icke Guide to the Global Conspiracy

I listened to David Icke speak in the 1990's in Brisbane, Australia. I remember him showing slides using an old projector to project photos onto a large screen. The room was small with few people. Years later, I was present when he spoke to a large audience at the Brisbane Entertainment Centre. And, then again at the Entertainment Centre on the Gold Coast where he spoke to thousands and received standing ovation after standing ovation. However, his visit in 2019 was 'banned' by the Australian Jackboots. Some say that the Australian right to speak died at that time, however, perhaps it was just coming into public awareness that 'free speech' had been under threat for a long time.

ISERBYT, CHARLOTTE THOMSON

The Deliberate Dumbing Down of America – A Chronological Paper Trail

Using personal experience, historical and policy documents, Ms Iserbyt (26 October, 1930 – 8 February, 2022) explains how powerful forces have manipulated the American school system since the 1950's. This brought about change from a knowledge based to a performance based system and from a free individualistic economy to a socialist-collectivised planned economy.

This book gives insight into how Change Agents are trained and infiltrate systems such as education to subtly change values and eliminate opposition. In the case of children this is the influence of parents.

JI, SAYER

Regenerate

"This book is a revolution. It goes way beyond the beliefs that have fuelled modern pharmaceutical medicine for decades and gives you all the science you will ever need to prove there is another way," said Christiane Northrup MD.

KENNEDY JR, ROBERT F

The Real Anthony Fauci: Big Pharma's Global War on Democracy, Humanity and Public Health
  Crimes Against Nature
  Thimerosal
  The evidence supporting the immediate removal of mercury - a known neurotoxin - from vaccines.
  Vax-Unvax – Let the Science Speak
  Co-author: Dr Brian Hooker, PhD PE
  A summary of studies found with a 'vax-unvax' comparison: children who had received all shots according to the vaccine schedule and those who were unvaccinated or unvaccinated during the first year of life. Dr Hooker said, "Overwhelmingly, the unvaccinated children were much healthier in terms of chronic illnesses, ailments as well as infectious disease."
  The book also addresses regulatory agencies recommending the Covid-19 shot to pregnant women without supporting data.

MATADOR FILMS

Uninformed Consent
  A powerful documentary by Matador Films – exposing massive deception, cruelty and genocide imposed upon humanity by the Global Elites.
  Directed by Todd Harris.

MIKOVITS, JUDY

HECKENLIVELY, KENT

The Truth About Masks
  "Keep your immune system healthy, don't ever wear a mask, because that cripples your own immune system."
  Plague of Corruption: Restoring Faith in the Promise of Science
  Dr Judy Mikovits has a PhD in Biochemistry and Molecular Biology. Her story from being a renowned scientist to having everything taken

from her and sitting in a gaol cell (no charges were laid) is told in this book. This happened when she discovered the inconvenient truths that animal and human foetal tissue used in vaccines/treatments against viruses was causing devastating plagues of chronic illness in human populations.

"Infection by injection," she says.

MIKOVITS, JUDY,

RUSCETTI, FRANCIS W,

HECKENLIVELY, KENT

Ending Plague

Dr Mikovits says, "The biggest thing our books tell you is that, "Never again get another injection and we, as a world, will experience health."

MIHALCEA, ANA MARIA

Light Medicine: A New Paradigm – The Science of Light, Spirit and Longevity

A modal for connecting light and spirit with the physical body, how our thoughts affect our health, wellbeing and your physical reality.

1921 winner of the Independent Press Award.

Dr Mihalcea said, "The fear of death is an illusion that inhibits us in our own spiritual journey."

Transhuman – Volume 1 – The Real COVID-19 Agenda

Transhuman – Volume 2 – overcoming the Global Depopulation Agenda

Dr Edward Group, Founder of Global Healing and the Global Healing Institute said, "I believe Dr Ana Mihalcea's book, Transhuman, is a vital wake-up call for those seeking to understand what is happening behind the scenes of transhumanism. Packed with essential information that is often overlooked or misunderstood, it serves as a crystal guide for anyone who values freedom, health, and the sanctity of the human soul."

Dr Ana Maria Mihalcea pays tribute to the work of Clifford Carnicom. When exploring the Carnicom website, I was overwhelmed by the dedication and love for humanity shown by Clifford and Carol Carnicom. Humanity will triumph because this Spirit, alive and well, also resides within the hearts of many.

NORTHRUP, CHRISTIANE

Mother-Daughter Wisdom: Creating a Legacy of Emotional and Physical Health
  The Wisdom of Menopause
  Women's Bodies, Women's Wisdom
  Goddesses Never Age
  Dodging Energy Vampires
  Beautiful Girl

Christiane Northrup MD, FACOG, is board-certified in obstetrics and gynaecology and integrative holistic medicine says, "When we find the connection between our thoughts, beliefs, physical health and life circumstances, we find that we are in the driver's seat of our lives and can make profound changes. Nothing is more exhilarating or empowering."

PAWLOWSKI, ARTUR

Lions Do Not Bow: The Unbreakable Courage of Canada's Pastor

Dr Bryan Ardis said, "Your book is going to keep people prepared and give them the tools and faith they need to stand firmly for every breach of freedom that is coming."

Pastor Pawlowski said, "I see us as a family and family sticks together, family works together, family helps each other. This was stolen from the world over the last four years so again, we must do the opposite."

PETERS, STEW

Died Suddenly

Steve Kirsh said in this 2022 film that if people knew what was in these 'vaccines', they would freak out. Karen Kingston agreed after her thousands of hours of research into official documents. Embalmer and Funeral Director Richard Hirschman is featured. He was one of the first to reveal the strange fibrous clots he was routinely finding in bodies and never seen before. Nicky Rupright King, is another embalmer speaking about the strange blood clots found in the veins of those who had been vaccinated.

Final Days

Producer, Stew Peters. Directors, Mathew Miller Skow and Nicholaus Stumphauzer.

A documentary to shed light on the contents in the Covid-19 injections and what these technologies do to the human body.

Watch The Water

A documentary produced by Stew Peters.

Dr Bryan Ardis brought the world's attention to venom-based synthetic spike protein genes wrapped in DNA plasmids found in the SARS-coV-2 jabs. He said that Covid symptoms can correlate to symptoms caused by king cobra and Chinese krait snake venom and other poisonous snakes.

It has been known since the 1980's that nicotine in tobacco plants is the perfect antidote to all snake venom on Earth.

His research suggests that because venom peptides bind to nicotinamide receptors in the body, nicotine in its pure form is proving to be a natural medicine for humanity. Nicotine receptors are to be found on every cell in the body. Nicotine is not addictive and indigenous cultures used tobacco medically for thousands of years. Placing the leaves on open sores or on a snake bite is well known. Inhaling the smoke for headaches and sinus problems is 'old' medicine. Nicotine is found in natural food such as eggplant, celery, tomatoes, potatoes and cauliflower.

Dr Ardis when being interviewed on A Right To Know by Sherry B said that nicotine has been scientifically shown to assist with Parkinson's disease, Alzheimer's disease, MS, type '1' diabetes, hyperthyroidism, myocarditis, ulcerative colitis, arthritis and autism.

What does virus mean in Latin – 'Snake Venom Poisoning'.

Research, the science, the case studies and how to use nicotine patches and presentations on the Dr Ardis Show website. Dr Ardis said, "One hundred percent of you have been lied to about the potential healing benefits of nicotine. They don't want you knowing that God put on the Earth in our plants a curative agent for the majority of our diseases."

His book, *Moving Beyond the Covid-19 Lies: Restoring Health & Hope for Humanity* tells the story and reveals shocking truths about Covid and the vaccines. Read it. It will set you free, said Dr Christiane Northrup.

SCHEIBNER, VIERA

Vaccination One Hundred Years of Orthodox Research
Behavioural Problems in Childhood: the link to vaccination

Dr Viera Scheibner PhD, when speaking on the Australian documentary by Bronwyn Hancock published in 1998, called *Vaccination: The Hidden Truth* said that it took almost three years of research before they looked at each other and said, 'Vaccines are killing babies'. And, also said that it is a well-documented fact that the incidence of mortality from infectious disease fell by ninety percent well before any vaccination was even introduced.

I met Dr Viera Scheibner in the 1990's. This warrior has been in the 'fight' for a very long time as one of the earliest to campaign and present research on the dangers of the childhood vaccines.

SENEFF, STEPHANIE

Toxic Legacy

How the Weedkiller Glyphosate is Destroying Our Health and The Environment – the *Silent Spring* of our time.

From an MIT scientist, mounting evidence that the active ingredient in the world's most-commonly-used weedkiller is responsible for debilitating chronic diseases, including autism, liver disease, and more.

SMITH, JEFFREY

Genetic Roulette – The Documented Health Risks of Genetically Engineered Foods Based on research, a chilling reminder that the effects of GM foods on human health are largely untested.

Seeds of Deception – Exposing Industry and Government Lies about the Safety of the Genetically Engineered Foods You're Eating.

SOL, JOSH DE

Take Back Your Power
  Smart meter documentary (2017)
Investigating current utility and government programmes involving mass in-home surveillance, eroding rights and causing harm in the name of 'smart' and 'green'.

STAPLETON, JOHN

Hideout in the Apocalypse
  Dark Policing
  Australia Breaks Apart
  FAILURE Family Law Reform Australia
John Stapleton, award winning journalist spanning over fifty years, is now reporting on the Covid era in Australia through his books and *A Sense of Place Magazine*. This is a place where the voice of the everyday Australian can be heard.

TENPENNY, SHERRI

Saying No to Vaccines: A Resource Guide for All Ages
A most comprehensive guide explaining how and why vaccines are detrimental to you and your child's health. This book offers an in-depth examination of how saying 'No' to vaccines can save your life and your child's life.

Fowl! Bird Flu: It's Not What you think
An investigative report into how dioxin, persistent organic pollutants (POPs), environmental chemicals and industrial chicken farming are contributing to the illness of migratory birds, chickens

and humans, making them more susceptible to the influenza virus called 'bird flu'.

Vaccines: The Risks, the Benefits, the Choices, a Resource Guide for Parents

This comprehensive guide is a great resource for those looking for facts and research to support their decision not to vaccinate.

Dr Sherri Tenpenny has been educating people world-wide on the dangers of the childhood vaccine schedule for decades. When interviewing her on the *Stew Peters Show* on 6 July, 2021, Stew Peters said: "Your bravery is noble."

Dr Tenpenny is an osteopathic medical doctor, board certified in three medical specialities. From 1986 to 1998, she was an Emergency Medicine physician and the director of the Emergency Department in Findlay, Ohio. Dr Tenpenny is regarded as the most articulate and knowledgeable physician on vaccine injuries.

I remember when Dr Tenpenny's speaking tour to Australia was cancelled due to threats to her life. This was 2015 and I wonder how many children's health situations would be different today if her human right of 'free speech' had not been taken away by the Australian Jackboots.

WAKEFIELD, ANDREW

Vaxxed

From cover-up to catastrophe (2016).

Vaxxed II

The People's Truth (2019).

1986: The Act (2020)

The Act is the story of what is behind the catastrophic situation we now find ourselves in, signed by Ronald Reagan in 1986 giving pharmaceutical companies indemnity from damage done by the recommended childhood vaccines.

Infertility: A Diabolical Agenda (2022)

Executive Producer, Robert F Kennedy Jr. This is a true story about a mass sterilisation agenda that took place in Africa over many years under the guise of a public health tetanus vaccination programme under the World Health Organisation.

AUTHOR'S STORY

Christmas 2021, I was given Sophie Scholl's writings and at the same time, I was writing up information from a Jonathan Otto's documentary for friends who did not have the time to listen to this valuable information. Over the years of being a yoga teacher, I had endeavoured to do this through newsletters for my students. And, then came the light bulb moment, "I am writing a book!"

"Oh, no, no way am I going to write about Covid!"

You know what they say, "Tell God your plans and he will laugh."

And, I remembered a poem I had written in 2012 that seemed relevant to this time in history. I was writing children's stories at the time and Thought *No-one will ever see what I had written!* I also wrote snippets of information that are relevant to this time in history and these have been included in the book. The seeding for The Jackboots took place and I carried on writing with no thought of a future outcome.

We all have stories to tell and our life's journey is always the perfect 'qualification'. Snippets of my childhood whilst living in the post war era dropped into the writing, as did my mum's stories of her experience living through The Great Depression and the Second World War. The emergence of the pharmaceutical companies into Australia and the disappearance of farmland were part of my lived experience.

The skills I learnt to become a secretary were important when in my latter years, I began to write. Children's stories I thought and I did, but was prompted to write memoirs, the first on our family's experience when coping with a child with addiction and mental health issues. The second one was my journey through breast cancer and pulling together allopathic and natural medicine to enjoy the following decade of excellent health that was not envisaged at the time of my diagnosis. It was through this time that intense researching began and I 'met' online, some that I have written about in this story. And, the third story, my experience of living through the Covid era.

Having a retail outlet in the nineteen-nineties with a focus on health and wellbeing was where I was awakened to the Giant's agenda. I lived through divorce, bringing up a family on my own and decades of experiencing my daughter's slide into the underworld. I caught glimpses of the darkside and I grew in strength. A qualified yoga teacher and founder of the Citrine School of Yoga, I believe that yoga is the cornerstone to how I dealt with this experience by learning to still and strengthen the mind among other techniques that have been invaluable. Exploring the field of astrology also brought insights and knowledge (qualified Practitioner of Astrology (FAA), Diploma in Psychological Astrology).

The years of study to become a holistic counsellor (Diploma in Counselling and Communication, Advanced Diploma in Holistic Counselling, Graduate Certificate in Artistic Therapies) took my awareness to another level. Focusing on emotional literacy and body-based techniques such as art, clay and sand brought an understanding of the trauma held within the body.

My love of books is another piece of the puzzle. As a child, I always had my nose in a book and a great passion for learning, searching and experiencing outside of my everyday life.

I believe my journey through life has enabled me to write about the unfolding of the Covid story I give to you in the hope that it may bring a little understanding, compassion and light into the process of moving forward towards a new and uplifting way of being.

Much Love Robyn
(Swami Ruchi Ananda)

"The whole universe and everything in it is alive in the sense of having love and its own dignified entity. The so-called inanimate and inorganic parts of nature have dignified life force. There is love and entity in the earth, air, rocks, water, everything, and some can see and feel it. No man has more-or-less spirit – we develop it more or less – use it more or less – are aware of it more-or-less, or not at all."
Peter Legh, 1978

REFERENCE LIST

Adams, M (2022) Canadian Government Resorts to Financial Terrorism Against Peaceful Convoy Protesters Demonstrating, Why We The People Can Never Trust Banks (or fiat), 15 February. Available at https://www.naturalnews.com/2022-02-15-canadian-government-resorts-to-financial-terrorism-against-peaceful-protesters.html# Accessed: 16 February, 2022.

Adams, M (2022) Dr Carrie Madej Post-Plane Crash Update With the Health Ranger, 26 July. Available at: https://forbiddenknowledgetv.net/dr-carrie-madej-post-plane-crash-update-with-the-health-ranger/

AFL Solicitors available at https://www.aflsolicitors.com.au

AHPRA (2021) Registered health practitioners and students: What you need to know about the COVID-19 vaccine rollout, 9 March. Available at https:www//ahpra.gov.au/News/2021-03-09-vaccination.

Altman, P (2023) Australian Government Exposed, 25 May. Available at https://phillipaltman.substack.com/p/australian-government-exposed. Accessed: 23 November, 2023.

AMPS (2022) A Time of COVID, 9 August. Available at https://AMPS.redunion.au.

AMPS (2022) Discussions from the Frontline with Peter Fam, Human Rights Lawyer, with Kara Thomas, 9 August. Available at: https://amps.redunion.com.au/news/episode-10-discussions-from-the-frontline-with-peter-fam.

Aparicio-Alonso M, Torres-Solorzano V, Mendex-Contreras J F, Acevedo-Whitehouse K, (2023) Scanning electron microscopy and EDX spectroscopy of commercial swabs used for COVID-19 lateral flow testing. Toxics, 11(10), 805: https://doi.org/10.3390/toxics11100805.

Aranya, Dasma-Mata (1994) October (reprint of talk given in 1971 - verbatim). The Aranya Ashram.

Aranya, Dasma-Mata (2006) June, Discernment and Intuition, (paper). The Aranya Ashram.

Ardis, B. The Dr Ardis Show, free patient resources for nicotine. Available at https://thedrardisshow.com/free-patient-resources – https://thedrardisshow.com/free-patient-resources/nicotine.pdf.

Ardis, B (2023) Interview with Dr Buttar on the upcoming Advanced Medical Conference, Episode - 05-03-2023. Available at: https://thedrardisshow.com/episode-05-03-2023-interview-with-dr-buttar-on-the-upcoming-advanced-medical-conference.

Ardis, B (2024) Artur Pawlowski and his book, Lions Do Not Bow. The Unbreakable Courage of Canada's Pastor, Episode 10-17-2024. Available at https://thedrardisshow.com/episode-10-17-2024-artur-pawlowski-and-his-book lions-do-not-bow.

A Right to Know, Art#251 Sherry B and Dr Bryan Ardis - The Hidden Truth and Lies About Nicotine and Much More! Available at https://rumble.com/v4jc7b8-artk251-sherry-b-and-dr-bryan-ardis-the-hidden-truth-and-lies-about-nicotine-and-much-more.

A Statement on Virus Isolation (Sovi) (2021) S Morell Fallen, T Cowan, A Kaufman. Available at: https://andrewkaufmanmd.com/sovi.

Australian Medical Professionals Society (AMPS), Too Many Dead, An Enquiry Into Australia's Excess Mortality. Available at https://mps.redunion.com.au/too-many-dead?utm-source=substack&utm-medium=email. Accessed: 4 December, 2023.

Bailey, M (2022) A Farewell to Virology (Expert Edition), 15 September. Available at: https://drsambailey.com/a-farewell-to-virology-expert-edition/ Accessed: 6 October, 2022.

Baletti, B (2023) Watch: CHD'S Brian Hooker Talks 'Vax-Unvax' with Kim Iversen, 31 August. Available at https://

childrenshealthdefense.org/defender/brian-hooker-talks-vax-unvax-with-kim-iversen.

Bhakdi, S (2023) Dangers of RNA - Vaccines. Available at: https://www.kla.tv/Coronavirus-en/27750&autoplay. Accessed: 13 January, 2023.

Billboard Battalion available at https://billboardbattalion.com/.

BioInitiative 2012, A Rationale for Biologically-based Exposure Standards for

low-Intensity Electromagnetic Radiation. Available at https://bioinitiative.org.

Bollinger, T and C (2015) The Truth About Cancer, A Global Quest Transcripts, Episode 1.

Bollinger, T and C (2016) The Truth About Cancer, Hay House Australia Pty Ltd.

Bollinger, T and C (2022) Propaganda Exposed: The Truth About Cancer, 4-11 May.

Available at https://go2.propagandaexposed.com/docuseries/episode-1/ Accessed: 6 May, 2022.

Bollinger, T and C (2023), The Truth About Vaccines Presents Remedy, Available at https://go2.remedy/film episodes 2 and 5. Accessed: 28 July 2023.

Brand, R (2022) The Truth About the Dutch Farmers Protest, Vandana Shiva in Conversation with Russell Brand, 13 July. Available at https://truthcomestolight.com. Accessed: 25 July 2022.

Breggin, P and G (2022) Farmers Fight Back - Tractor Blockades, Burning Bales of Hay and Animal Manure Showers, 10 July. Available at https://gingerbreggin.substack.com/p/farmers-fight-back-tractor-blockage. Accessed: 20 July, 2022.

Brighthope, I (2024) We owned the world's news, we owned (controlled) the facts ..., 26 January. Available at https//ianbrighthope.substack.com/p/we-owned-the-world's-news-we-owned-(controlled)-the-facts. Accessed: 27 January, 2024.

Brogan, K (2019) Own Your Self, Hay House Australia Pty Ltd.

Buckley, B (2010) Transition Farms, Castelen Press, Mount Tamborine.

Buttar, R A available at https://www.askdrbuttar.com.

Café Locked Out (2023) Kulture Ep 01 Songs. Available at https://cafelockeddown.substack.com/p/culture/ep-01-songs. Accessed 9 November, 2023.

Café Locked Out (2023) Kaleb The Rise of a Young Lion and a Tribute to Dazelle. Available at https://substack.com/home/post/p-145495719.

Cairns News (2022) Riccardo Bossi Thanks All Australia for Canberra Successful Rally, 13 February. Available at https://rumble.com/vusxoo-riccardo-bossi-thanks-all-australia-for-canberra-successful-rally-outcome.html. Accessed: 12 February, 2022.

Cairns News (2022) Gold Coast Covid Ward Empty For Months While Vaxx Casualties Stream In, 15 March. Available https://cairnsnews.org/2022/03/1/15/gold-coast- ward- empty-for-months-while-vaxx-casualties-stream-in/ Accessed: 16 March, 2022.

Cairns News (2022) Aussie Doctor Blows Whistle On Entire Covid Scamdemic At Covid Medical Network Seminar, 2 September. Available at https://cairnsnews.org.2022/09/2-aussie-doctor-blows-whistle-on-entire-covid-scamdemic-at-covid-medical-network-seminar/.

Cairns News (2022) Never use corrupt GofundMe again, use GiveSendCo, 6 February by Alexander Bruce, US correspondent. Available at cairnsnews.org/2022/02/06/never-use-corrupt-gofundme-again-use-givesendco.

Cairns News (2022) Get to Canberra Rally by Saturday Plenty of Food and Camping Spaces, 10 February. Available at https://cairnsnews.org/2022/02/10/get-to-canberra-rally-by-saturday-plenty-of-food-and-camping-spaces/

Capuzzo, M (2023) New Report: Young People Dying of Cancer at 'Explosive' Rates, UK Government Data Show, 21 November. Available at https://childrenshealthdefense.org/defender/young-people-dying-of-cancer-at-explosive-rates- Accessed: 11 December, 2023.

Carnicom Institute. Available at https://carnicominstitute.substack.com.

Carnicom Institute, 100 Countermeasures for Targets of Electronic Harassment by Leslie Oliver. Available at https://carnicom-institute.org/meditation-100-countermeasures-for--for-targets-of-electronic-harassment-by-leslie-oliver.

Cavendish, L (2019) The Lost Lands, Blue Angel Publishing, Glen Waverley, Australia.

Centre for Countering Digital Hate (2021) The Disinformation Dozen, 24 March. Available at: https://counterhate.com/research/the-disinformation-dozen.

Children's Health Defense Team (2022) CDC Denounces Violence in Brussels After Police Disrupt COVID Mandates Rally, 26 January. Available at https://childrenshealthdefense.org/defender/chd-denounces-violence-brussels-covid-mandates-rally/

Children's Health Defense, 'Friday Roundtable' (2022) Enough is Enough, Doctors Send Warning to Parents as FDA Nears EUA of Covid Shots for Under 5, 4 June. Available at: https://live.childrenshealthdefense.org/shows/chd-friday-roundtable.

Children's Health Defense (2022) What's Going on With Women's Cycles? Everything You Need to Know About COVID Vaccine Shedding with Dr. Brian Hooker, 9 June. Available at https://live.childrenshealthdefense.org/shows/good-morning-chd/nnhEojOx-u.

Children's Health Defense (2022) Young Man Sues Merck, Wants Accountability For Injuries Caused by Gardasil HPV Vaccine, 3 November. Available at https://childrenshealthdefense.org/defender/merrick-brunker-merck-lawsuit-gardasil-hpv-vaccine, 21 July.

Children's Health Defense Team (2023) RFK Jr Proves HHS is in Violation of "Mandate for Safer Childhood Vaccines" as Stipulated in the Vaccine Injury Compensation Act, 21 July. Available at https://childrenshealthdefense.org.

Children's Health Defense TV (2023) Militarized Healthcare, 16 March. Available at https://live.childrenshealthdefense.org/chd-tv/shows.

Chile's President Speech on 5G: Machines to Read and Insert Thoughts, 15 June, 2021. Available at https://odysee.com/@ExtraCynical:1/chile-president-5G-machines-to-read-and-insert-thoughts.

Chlubek, D and Sikora, M (2020) Fluoride and the Pineal Gland, Appl. Sci. 2020. 10(8), 2885: https://doi.org/10.3390/app10082885.

Coleman, V (2022) Doctors and Nurses Betrayed Patients and Themselves, 22 September. Available at https://vernoncoleman.org/articles/doctors-and-nurses-betrayed-patients-and-themselves. Accessed: 26 September, 2022.

Connett P, Beck J and Micklem (2010) The Case Against Fluoride, White River Junction: Chelsea Green Publishing Company.

Constitution Watch (2023) Maori Government prosecutes four high-ranking New Zealand officials for committing crimes in response to the covid pandemic, 27 October. Available at https://constitutionwatch.com.au/maori-government-prosecutes-four-high-ranking-new-zealand-officials-for-committing-crimes-in-response-to-the-covid-pandemic.

Corona Extra-Parliamentary Inquiry Committee available at https://acu2020.org.

Corona Investigative Committee available at https://odysee.com/@Corona-Investigative-Committee:5.

Corona Committee Findings Summary available at https://odysee.com/@Corona-Investigative-Committee:5/Reiner-Fuellmich.

Covid Medical Network available at https://covidmedicalnetwork.com.

Covid Medical Network (2021) Covid Medical Network Letter to Doctors and Health Professionals, 6 August. Available at https://constitutionwatch.com.au/covid-medical-network-letter-to-doctors-and-health-professionals.

Covid Medical Network (2021) Medical Terrorism Is Unacceptable, 10 November. Available at https://covidmedicalnetwork.com/cmn-updates/dr-mark-hobart-raided.aspx.

Covid Medical Network (2022) Open Letter to AGI, TGA and Federal Department of Health, 8 March. Available at https://covidmedicalnetwork.com/open/letters/open-letter-to-atagi.aspx.

Crook, P (2020) Thank You for listening, Peter Crooke, North Tamborine, Qld, Australia.

Debt-Stop (2022) Truth-Speaking Doctor Blows Up AMA Conference, 2 August, Available at https://debtstop.com.au/tag/dr-bay/

Dr Tenpenny's Eye on the Evidence (2023) with special guest, Eric Nepute DC, 27 December. Available at https://drtenpenny.substack.com/p/morning-coffee-dr-nepute.

Druda, A (2009) The Tao of Rejuvenation, Darma Café books, California.

Elijah, S (2023) The Veil of Silence Over Excess Deaths, 26 October. Available at https://brownstone.org.articles/veil-of-silence-over-excess-deaths. Accessed: 21 November, 2023.

Emoto, M (2005) Hidden Messages in Water, Atria Books, New York

Environmental International, Volume 146, January 2021. Published by Elsevier: Ragusa A, Svelato A, Santacroce C, Catalano P, Notarstefano V, Carnevali O, Papa F, et al. Plasticenta: first evidence of microplastics in human placenta, https://doi.org/10.1016/j.envint.2020.106274.

Evans, M (2021) Soil: the incredible story of what keeps the earth, and us, healthy. Murdock Books, Crows Nest, Australia.

Evans, M and Rodger, I (2000) Healing for Body Soul and Spirit. First printed by Thorson, an Imprint of HarperCollins Publishers, Great Britain. This edition was published by Floris Books.

Exley C. Why industry propaganda and political interference cannot disguise the inevitable role played by human exposure to a minimum degree in degenerative disease including Alzheimer's disease - Front Neurol. 2014 Oct 27;5:212: https://doi.org/10.3389/fneur.2014.00212.

Exley, C (2024) Vaccine Advice to Parents, 2 February. Available at https://drchristopherexley.substack.com/p/vaccine-advice-to-parents. Accessed: 8 February, 2024. (Published with permission).

Exposing the Darkness Newsletter, The Lioness of Judah Ministry (2023), New Zealand Whistleblower Facing 7 Years in Prison for Exposing Massive Vax Deaths, 7 December. Available at https://lionessofjudah.substack.com/p/new-zealand-whistleblower-facing-7-years-in-prison-for-exposing-massive-vax-deaths. Accessed: 8 December, 2023.

Farrow, L (2013) The Iodine Crises: What You Don't Know About Iodine Can Wreck Your Life. New York: Devon Press.

Firstenberg, A (1997) Microwaving Our Planet: The Environmental Impact of the Wireless Revolution, Published by Cellular Phone Taskforce. Available at https://www.cellphonetaskforce.org/wp-content/uploads/2022/05/Microwaving_Our_Planet_firstenberg.pdf. Accessed: 27 September, 2022.

Fischer, D (2009) How to Fight Cancer and Win. Toorak: Bookman Health

Fisher, B L (2015) The Health Liberty Revolution to Save Our Children, 28 October. Available at https://www.nvic.org/newsletter/oct-2015/the-health-liberty-revolution-to-save-our-children. Accessed: 7 October, 2022.

Fluoride Free Peel, https://www.fluoridefreepeel.ca/stefan-lanka-resources/

Forest of the Fallen, available at: https://theforestofthefallen.com/.

Forest of the Fallen Founder, Australia (2023) 16 September. Available at https://odysee.com/@forestofthefallen:6/FotFwithD;2.

FreeNZ (2023) M.O.A.R. (Mother Of All Revelations), The Irrefutable Data on New Zealand's Excess Deaths From The Covid Jabs, 30 November. Available at https://freenz.substack.com/p/moar-mother-of-all-revelations. Accessed: 5 December, 2023.

Fuellmich, R (2021) Reiner Fuellmich Interviews Tony Nicolic, Sydney Lawyer, 12 August. Available at: https://worldfreedomalliance.org/au/news/reiner-fuellmich-interviews-tony-nikolic-sydney-lawyer/ Accessed: 15 August, 2021.

Fuellmich, R (2021) Reiner Fuellmich Interviews Funeral Director John O'Looney, 20 October. Available at: https://Odyssey.comQTheGrcatReset:7/reiner-fuellmich-funeral-director-john-o'looney.

Fuellmich, R (2022) Dr Reiner Fuellmich - Opening Statement to a Grand Jury on Crimes Against Humanity Nuremberg 2.0. Available at https://www.bitchute.com/video/CAW6K2fLhv2j/

Fuellmich, R (2023) International Crimes Investigative Committee (ICIC), Barrie Trower With Dr Reiner Fuellmich: 5G/Microwave as a Weapon (Part 2), 29 February. Available at https://truthcomestolight.com/barrie-trower-with-dr-reiner-fuellmich. Accessed: 20 January, 2023.

Gabbard, T (2022) There are 25+ US-funded biolabs in Ukraine, 13 March. Available at https://www.youtube.com/watch?v=5YflOtJw6fO.

Garcia, E (2022) The Catastrophic Experience in New Zealand, 18 July. Available at https://www.globalresearch.ca/responsibility-choice/5787009. Accessed: 23 July, 2022.

Gentempo. P (2022) EndGame 9 Part Series, Available at https//endgameseries.com/viewing/. Accessed, 15 March, 2022.

Global Research (2020) Why Germany's Corona Extra-Parliamentary Inquiry Committee Is Necessary? Dr Heiko Schoning, 28 September. Available at https://www.globalresearch.ca/

Good Morning CHD (2022) Episode 48: What's Going On With Women's Cycles? Everything You Need to Know About Covid Vaccine Shedding With Dr Brian Hooker, 9 June. Available at https://live.childrenshealthdefense.org/shows/good-morning-chd/nnhEojOx-u.

Grand Jury, The Court of Public Opinion (2022) https://www.grand-jury.net. – https://grandjurythecourtofpublicopinion.com.

Group, E (2024) Healing for the AGES Virtual Masterclass Replay. Available at https://healingfortheages.com/?utm-source=drip&utm. Accessed: 2 March, 2024.

Hahn, Maija, C (2022) Instead of Admitting Mask Mandates Harm Kids, CDC Lowers Expectations for Speech. Available at https://childrenshealthdefense.org/defender/cdc-lowers-expectations-for-speech-development. Accessed: 8 March, 2022.

Harvard Pilgrim Health Care, Inc. 2/01/07-09/30/10. Electronic Support for Public Health Vaccine Adverse Event Reporting System. Available at https://digital.ahrq.gov/.../r18hs017045-lazarus-final-report-2011.pdf · PDF file. Accessed: 23 June, 2022.

Hawkins, D1 (1998) Power Versus Force, Hay House Australia Pty Ltd, Brighton-Le-Sands, NSW, Australia.

Health Freedom Summit, (2022) Categories/Day 1 - Health - Stephanie Seneff PhD: Covid-19 Vaccines and Neurodegenerative Disease. Accessed: 14 March, 2022.

Ho, M-W (2013) The New Genetics and Natural Versus Artificial Genetic Modification, Entropy, 15(11), 47-48-4781.

Hooker B S, Miller N Z. Analysis of health outcomes in vaccinated and unvaccinated children. Developmental delays, asthma, ear infections and gastrointestinal disorders: Available at https://doi.org/10.1177/2050312120925344.

Hooker B S, Miller N Z. Health effects in vaccinated versus unvaccinated children, with covariates for breastfeeding status and type of birth: Available at https://doi.org/10.15761/JTS.1000459.

Howe, L M (2000) British Cell Phone Safety Alert and an Interview with Robert O Becker, MD. Available at www.energyfields.org/science/becker.

Huff, E (2022) Dutch Government to Seize 600 Farms at Gunpoint, Claiming Nitrogen is a Pollutant, 19 October. Available at https://www.newstarget.com. Accessed: 21 October, 2022.

ICAN Legal Update (2023) ICAN-Funded Lawsuit Prohibiting Any Local Vaccine Mandates Wins Final Battle; Sets California Precedent, 23 February. Available at www.icandecide.org. Accessed: 2 April, 2023.

ICAN Legal Update (2023) CDC and NIH Unable to Provide a Single Study to Support the Safety of Injecting Aluminium Adjuvants Despite its Widespread Use in Childhood Vaccines, 1 March. Available at www.icandecide.org. Accessed: 16 April, 2023.

ICIC.LAW (2024) Statement by Reiner Fuellmich, 15 July. Available at https://icic.law/en/videos.

Icke, D (2010) Human Race Get off Your Knees - The Lion Sleeps No More. David Icke Books Ltd, Isle of Wight, UK.

Igan, M (2023) The End Game - Launchpad Podcast, 17 July. Available at https://www:bitchute.com/video/EeUPnawioOng/.

International Electromagnetic Frequency Alliance (2016) Seletun Statement, 20 December. Available at https://www.iemfa.org/seletun-statement.

Jaku, Eddie (2020) The Happiest Man on Earth, Pan MacMillan Australia Pty Ltd.

Ji, S (2024) Giant in Natural Medicine, Dr Andrew Saul, 10 February. Available at https://greenmedinfo.com/blog/greenmedinfocom-mourning.

Johnson, R (2022) A Second Opinion on Covid, 4 February. Available at https://www.ronjohnson.senate.gov/2022/2/a-second-opinion-on-covid. Accessed: 23 March, 2022.

Kempton, B (2018), Wabi Sabi: Japanese Wisdom for a Perfectly Imperfect Life. Piatkus, An Imprint of Little, Brown Book Group, UK.

Kennedy, R F Jr (2015) Thimerosal - Let the Science Speak. Skyhorse Publishing Inc, New York.

Kennedy, R F Jr (2021) RFK Jr Addresses Louisiana Health and Welfare Committee, 8 December. Available at https://rumble.com/vqg9r5-rfk-jr-addresses-louisiana-health-welfare-committee.html.

Kessler, D (2019) Finding Meaning, Rider, an imprint of Ebury Publishing, London.

Killeen, B A (2024) The Most Unexpected Use for Your Everyday Onion, 18 March. Available at https://www.allrecipes.com/do-onions-work-as-air-purifiers.

Kingston, K (2023) Foreign US Biolabs Exposed! Russian General Igor Kirillov Cites Karen Kingston, 14 March. Available at https://www.bitchute.com/video/IOyEfrfBGIUF. Accessed: 10 April 2023.

Kingston, K (2023) It's Time to Blow the Lid Off the Global Health System, 23 June. Available at https://karenkingston.substack.com/its-time-to-blow-the-lid-off-the-global-health-system. Accessed: 5 July, 2023.

Kirsten, F (2023) Counteract Discussions: Episode 2 - Transhumanism, Wireless Body Area Networks, 12 December. Available at https://faiezkirsten.substack.com/p/counteract-discussion-episode-2-transhumanism-wireless-body-area-networks. Accessed: 14 December, 2023.

Klinghardt, D (2020) Light Vs Dark, Heavy Metals and Toxins, www.youtube.com/watcxh??v=zR6OiKNnp2M. Accessed: August 2022.

Korey, P. Dr Pierre Korey's Opening Address at the 2nd World Congress in Brazil. Available at https://rumble.com/v1b2ez9-dr-pierre-korys-opening-address-at-the-2nd-world-congress-in-brazil-june-3.html.

Lanka, S (2021) Health Freedom for Humanity, 23 April. Available at https://healthfreedomforhumanity.org/dr-stefan-lanka-virologist/

Latter-Day Media, (2020) International Doctors Declaring Freedom from Covid, 19 November. Available at https://vimeo.com/481390190. Accessed: September 2022.

Latypova, S available at https://www.sashalatypova.com.

Latypova, S (2023) Available at https://rumble.com/v2197ao-slobodni-podcast-10-sasha-latypova-pandemija-je-bila-vojna-demonstracija. Accessed: 7 May, 2023.

Leader, F (2024) Stop Lying About 5G, 6 April. Available at https://outlook.live.com/mail/O/inbox/id/AQQkAwATY3... LearnTheRisk.org.

Legh, P (1978) Simple Faith and Keeping it Simple, International Light, July-September, 1978.

Li X et al. Myocarditis Following COVID-19 BNT162b2 Vaccination Among Adolescents in Hong Kong. JAMA Pediatr. 2002 June 1;176(6):612-614: https://doi.org/10.1001/jamapediatric.2022.0101.

Longley, R (Updated 5 May 2020) Biography of Sophie Scholl, German Activist. Available at https://www.thoughtco.com/biography-of-sophie-scholl-4843206.

Love, A (2021) World Doctors Warning: Stay Away From The Vaxxed, 28 April. Available at https://ambassadorlove.wordpress.com/2021/04/28/world-doctors-warning-stay-away-from-the-vaxxed/ Accessed: 16 September, 2022.

Lurnpa (2022) Australian Aboriginal Leader Lurnpa: The Genocidal Land Grab in the Northern Territory (The Real agenda Behind the Unfolding Medical Tyranny),14 February. Available at:

https://truthcomestolight.com/australian-aboriginal-leader-lurnpa-on-the-genocidal-land-grab-in-the-northern-territories-the-real-agenda-behind-the-unfolding-medical-tyranny/.

Lyons-Weiler J, Thomas P. Relative Incidence of Office Visits and Cumulative Rates of Billed Diagnoses Along the Axis of Vaccination. Int J Environ Res Public Health 2020 Nov 22;17(22):8674: https://doi.org/10.3390/ijerph17228674.

Maarman, R (2022) Riccardo Maarman: South Africa's Court Case Dismissed -"Let's Go to Parliament" 8 April. Available by courtesy of Truth Comes to Light at: https://truthcomestolight.com/ricardo-maarman-south-africa-show-us-the-virus-court-case-dismissed-lets-go-to-parliament/ Accessed:10 April, 2022.

Madej, C. available at https://www.carriemadej.com.

Madej, C (2022) Dr Sherry Tenpenny and Dr Carrie Madej Video, 13 May. Available at https://gospelnetwork.org/2022/05/13-dr-sherry-tenpenny-and-dr-carrie-madej-video/ Available at: 22 August, 2022.

Marks, D (2022) Former BlackRock Advisor Tells RFK, Jr: 'FDA Is In On The Cover-Up.' 18 March. Available at https://childrenshealthdefense.org/defender/chd-tv-rfk-jr-defender-blackrock-edward-dowd-fda-cover-up/ Accessed: 19 March, 2022.

Massey, C (2021) 211 health/science institutions globally all failed to cite even 1 record of "SARS-COV-2" purification, by anyone, anywhere, ever, 6 June. Available at https://www.fluoridefreepeel.ca/68-health-science-institutions-globally-all-failed-to-cite-even-1-record-of-SARS-coV-2-purification-by-anyone-anywhere-ever/ Accessed: 13 October, 2021.

Massey, C. (2022) Declarations notarized. Available at https://www.fluoridefreepeel.ca/wp-content/12/2022-12-02-Christine-virus-FOIs-declaration-notarized-1-pfd.

Massey, C (2020) FOI files can be accessed at https://www.fluoridefreepeel.ca/wp-content-uploads/2020/10/FOI-and-formal-responses-re-covid19-virus-isolation-purification-from-19-institutions-Oct-10-2020.pdf.

Massey, C (2023) Official Evidence that Virology is Pseudoscience, 10 June. Accessed at https://bitchute.com/video/gvu4NbieSuVb/.

Massey, C (2024) More Danish "Experts" With No Scientific Evidence That "HPV" Exists Let Alone Causes Cancer: Statens Serum Institute, 3 April. Available at https://christinemasseyfois.substack.com. Accessed: 5 April, 2024.

McBean, E (1976) Swine Flu Expose, Health Research Books, WD Gann Inc.

Mead M, Seneff S, Wolfinger R, et al. (24 January, 2024) COVID-19 mRNA Vaccines: Lessons Learned from the Registrational Trials and Global Vaccination Campaign. Cureous 16(1):e52876: https://doi.org/10,7759/cureous.52876.

Mercola, J (2011) Sudden Death Syndrome: the hidden epidemic destroying your gut flora (online) Available at www.articles.Mercola.com/...2022/12/10/dr-don-huber-interview-part1.

Mihalcea, A M (2023) I Am Starting a New Freedom Movement - Humanity United, For the Preservation of the Human Species, 30 June. Available at https://anamihalceamdphd.substack.com/ Accessed: 1 July, 2023.

Mihalcea, A M (2023) Rubbery Clot Formation Shown In Living C19 Unvaccinated Person Via Darkfield Microscopy - Hydrogel Replacing Blood, 22 July. Available at https://anamihalceamdphd.substack.com/.

Mihalcea, A M (2023) Speeding Covid-19 Drug Discovery with Quantum Dots Available at https://anamihalceamdphd.substack.com/ Accessed: 26 August, 2023.

Mihalcea, A M (2023) Human Papilloma Virus Vaccine HPV for 9-12 Year Old Children Shows Nanobots, Self-Assembly Hydrogel and Polymer Mesh Development, 2 September. Available at https://anamihalceamdphd.substack.com/Accessed: 2 September, 2023.

Mihalcea. A M (2023) Measles, Mumps, Rubella and Varicella Vaccine Swarms, Quantum Dots and Self Assembly Hydrogel, 5 September. Available at https://anamihalceamdphd.substack.com/ Accessed: 7 September, 2023.

Miller N Z, Goldman, G S, (2011) Infant mortality rates regressed against the number of vaccine doses routinely given is there a biochemical or synergistic toxicity? Hum Exp Toxicol. 2011 Sep;30(9):1420-8. doi: 10.1177/0960327111407644. Epub 2011 May 4.

Murdoch, A (2021) Canadian Pastor Arrested in Highway Takedown After Holding Service Defying Lockdowns, 28 May. Available at https://www.lifesitenews.com/news/canadian-pastor-arrested-in-highway-takedown-after-holding-service-defying-lockdowns.

Murdoch, A (2022) Pastor Artur Pawlowski Describes Horrid Jail Conditions, Says He Is Still a Political Prisoner, 2 April. Available at https://www.lifesitenews.com/news/pastor-artur-Pawlowski-describes-horrid-jail-conditions-says-he-is-still-a-political-prisoner.

Nahmad, C (2008) Angel Healing. Watkins Publishing, London.

Nevison C. A comparison of temporal trends in United State autism prevalence to trend in suspected environmental factors. Environ Health 13, 73 (2014): https://doi.org/10.1186/1476-069X-13-73.

Vaccine Nevradakis, M (2022) Corporate Mandates and Vaccine Passports - Brought to You by BlackRock and Vanguard, 16 February. Available at https://childrenshealthdefense.org/defender/corporate-vaccine-mandates-and-vaccine-passports. Accessed: 27 February, 2022.

Nixon D. Available at https://davidnixon.substack.com.

Northrup, C (2023) Update on Myocarditis and Aviation With Josh Yoder of US Freedom Flyers, 11 September. Available at https://truenorthdr.substack.com/p/update-on-myocarditis. Accessed: 11 December, 2023.

Null, G (1996) Kary Mullis Full Interview, Gary Null Production. Available at https://rumble.com/v11jbtq-kary-mullis-full-interview-gary-null-productions.

NZDSOS (2022) Deaths Following Covid-19 Vaccination, 24 May. Available at: https://nzdsos.com/2022/05/24/deaths-following-c-19-vaccination/.

O'Bryan, T (2016) Autoimmune Fix, Rodale Inc. New York.

Orthomolecular Medicine News Service, June 1, 2022, Monkeypox Infection to fear or Not to Fear? Commentary by Thomas E Levy MD, JD. Available at https://orthomolecular.org/resources/omns/v18n17.shtml. Accessed: 2 June, 2022.

Orthomolecular Medicine News Service, 27 July, 2022, Why Australia Remains a Penal Colony for Physicians. Available at https://orthomolecular.activehosted.com/indes/php?action. Accessed: August 2022. (Published with permission).

Otto, J (2021) Vaccines Secrets: Reloaded.

Otto, J (2022) Covid Secrets: Reloaded, Available at https://concen.org/content/vaccine-secrets-reloaded-covid-crisis-2022-new-bonus-episodes-1-10.

Otto, J (2022) Unbreakable: Destined to Thrive, Episode 1-9, 31 May - 8 June. Available at https://unbreakableseries.com/episode-2. Accessed: 2 June, 2022.

Otto, J (2022) Unbreakable: Destined to Thrive Reloaded, Episode 1-9, 15 August. Available at https://unbreakableseries.com.

Otto, J (2022) Brave, Live Courageously, Heal Miraculously, 26 September. Available at https://braveseries.com.

Otto, J (2023) New Hope Series. Available at https://newhopeseries.com/episode-9-replay. Accessed: 9 May 2023.

Otto, J (2023) Disease In Reverse. Available at https://diseaseinreverse.com/episode-11-live/ Accessed: 6 July, 2023.

Otto, J (2023) Disease In Reverse. Available at https://diseaseinreverse.com/qa-replay/ 8 July, 2023.

Payeras, B. Available at: www.tomeulamo.com/fitxers/264_CORONA-5G-d.pdf .

Pall M (2018) Special Report on 5G,17 May. Available at https://www.emfcyprus.com/5G/and-martin-pall-report. Accessed: 18 July 2022.

Parotto T, Thorp J A, Hooker B, Mill P J , Newman J, Murphy L, et al. Covid-19 and The Surge in Decidual Cast Shedding: G Med ci. 2022; 3(1):107-117: https://www.doi.org/ 10.46766/thegms.pubheal.22041401.

Pauline Hanson's One Nation. Withdraw Gene-Based treatment – Covid Medical Network. https://www.onenation.org.au/with-experimental-gene-treatment-covid-medical-network.

Peters, S (2022) Died Suddenly. Available at https://www.imdb.com/title/tt23810972/.

Peters, S (2022) Watch The Water. Available at https://rumble.com/v1omd2r-world-premier-watch-the-water.html.

Public Health and Medical Professionals for Transparency (2021) 5.3.6 Cumulative Analysis of Post-Authorisation Adverse Event Reports of PF-07302048 (BNY162B2) Received Through 28 February 2021. Available at: https://phmpt.org/wp-content/uploads/2021/11/5.3.6.-postmarketing-experience.pdf.

Planetlockdown (2022) Planet Lockdown Series, Dr Peter McCullough Full Interview, 19 June. Available at https://rumble.com/v192brc-dr-peter-mccullough-full-interview-planet-lockdown-series.html. Accessed: 20 July 2022.

Prather, J. Meet Your Intelligence Officer, available at https://jeffreyprather.com.

Radiation Dangers (2020) Study Shows Direct Correlation between 5G Networks and "Coronavirus" Outbreaks, 24 April. Available at https://radiationdangers.com/2020/04/24/study-shows-direct-correlation-between-5g-networks-and-coronavirus-outbreaks.

Radical, (2022) Dr Mike Yeadon on Radical with Maajid Nawaz, 18 september. Available at https://rumble.com/v1kuat5-dr-mike-yeadon-interviewed-by-maajid-nawaz-on-building-back-better-first-by-destroying.

Rebel News (2022) NZ Police Clash with Anti-mandate Protestors Outside Parliament, 2 March. Available at https://www.rebel-news.com/nz-police-clash-with-anti-mandate-protests-outside-parliament. Accessed: 8 March, 2022.

Rich The Renegade (2022) The Real Truth About Health: A Natural Way to Get Electricity Supplied to The Body in A Healthy Way And Why It Matters, Stephanie Seneff - Interview. Available at https://www.its.health/a-natural-way-to-get-electricity-supplied-to-the-body-in-a healthy-way-and-why-it-matters/ Accessed: 30 May, 2022.

Roberts, M (2022) Covid Under Question, Mr Julian Gillespie, 25 March. Available at https://rumble.com/vyb02m-covid-under-question-mr-julian-gillespie.html.

Roberts, M (2022) The COVID Inquiry 2.0, 17 August. Available at https://www.malcolmrobertsqld.com.au/the-covid-enquiry-2.0. Accessed: 29 January, 2024.

Ryan, A (2022) Russia drops massive evidence of Ukranian and US bio-labs onto the United Nation's lap, 16 November. Available at https://cairnsnews.org/2022/11/16/russia-drops-massive-evidence-of-ukranian-and-us-bio-labs-onto-the-united-nation's-lap.

Samsel A, and Seneff S. Journal of Biological Physics and Chemistry, March 2017

https://doi 017:https://doi.org/10.4024/25SA16A.jbpc.17.01.

Sanders, B (2014) available at: https://emilysquotes.com/2014/11/14. Accessed: 7 July, 2023.

Scott-Mumby, K. Dr Archie Kalokerinos available at https://alternativer-doctor.com/dr-archie-kalokerinos.

Schwab, K, Malleret, T (2020) Covid-19: The Great Reset, World Economic Forum, Switzerland.

Seneff, S (2021) Dr Stephanie Seneff: Covid-19 and Degenerative Disease, 3 January. Available at https://worldcouncilforhealth.org/multimedia/stephanie-seneff-covid-vaccines-disease

Seneff S, Nigh G. Worse than the Disease? Reviewing Some Possible Unintended Consequences of the mRNA Vaccine Against Covid-19, May 2021: https://doi.org/10.56098/ijvtpr.v2i1.23.

Sharav, V (2022) Holocaust Survivor: Never Again Is Now Unless We all resist, 25 January. Available at https://childrenshealthdefense.org/defender/vera-sharav. Accessed: 4 May 2022.

Sharav, V (2022) Nuremberg Code Is Our Defense Against Abusive Behaviour, 22 August. Available at https://childrenshealthdefense.org/defender-vera-sharav- Accessed: 2 September, 2022.

Shardlow E, Linhart C, Connor S, Softely E, Exley C. The measurement and full statistical analysis including Bayesian methods of the aluminium content of infant vaccines: https://doi.org/10.1016/jtemb.2021.126762.

Sharma, R (2021) The Everyday Hero *Manifesto*, Harper Collins Publishing, England.

Sherwood, P (2007) Holistic Counselling a New Vision for Mental Health, Sophia Publications, Western Australia.

Siri, A. FDA Buries Data On Seriously Injured. Available at https://aronsiri.substack.com/p/fda-buries-data-on-seriously-injured.

Siri, A (2022) Instead of FDA's Requested 500 Pages Per Month, Court Orders FDA to Produce Pfizer Covid-19 Data at Rate of 55,000 Pages Per Month, 6 January. Available at https://aaronsiri.substack.com.

Siri, A (2021) One Brave ICU Physician Reporting Covid-19 Injuries Leads to a Dozen More, 2 November. Available at https://aaronsiri.substack.com/p/one-brave-icu-physician-reporting, Accessed: 7 May, 2022.

Sophie Scholl Quotes - Goodreads, Available at https://www.goodreads.com/author/quotes/801549.Sophie_Scholl.

Sorensen, D (2021) Covid-19 Test Kits Imports by Country, Login Register WITS (World Integrated Trade Solution) 18 December. Available at https://stopworldcontrol.com/2017- covid19-test-kits.pdf.

Sorensen D, Zelenko V (2021) The Vaccine Death Report. Available at https://stopworldcontrol.com/downloads/en/vaccines/vaccinereport/pdf.

Sorensen, D (2022) Grand Jury, https://stopworldcontrol.com/downloads/GrandJurySummary1.pdf.

Sorensen, D (2022) Reiner Fuellmich: Encouraging update after false allegations. Available at https://stopworldcontrol.com.

Sorensen, D (2023) Maori Vs Plandemic, with Reiner Fuellmich and a group of attorneys and scientists. Available at https://stopworldcontrol.com/maori/.

Solum, C available at https://celestialreport.com.

Spittle, B (2008) Fluoride Fatigue, Dunnedine: Paua Press Limited.

Steiner, R (2014) The Balance in the World and Man, Lucifer and Ahriman GA 158. Available at: www.rsarchive.org.

Stevenson, S (2022) Light Ascension, Available at https://www.lightascention.com.

Stew Peters Show (2021) Dr Sherri Tenpenny Goes FULL TRUTH With Explosive Fact-Based Spew on 'Stew Peters Show', 6

July. Available at https://www.redvoicemedia.com/2021/07/dr-sherri-tenpenny-goes-full-truth-with-explosive-based-fact-spew-on-stew-peters-show/ Accessed: 22 June, 2022.

Stew Peters Show (2023) Transhumanism Threatens Humanity: mRNA Bioweapon Merges Human Biology With Digital Technology. Available at https://stewpeters.com/video/2023/06/transhumanism-threatens-humanity-mRNA-bioweapon-merges-human-biology-with-digital-technology. Accessed: 24 June, 2023.

Sun Tzu Quotes, Available at https://www.azquotes.com/quote/576159.

Taliano, M (2021) Help Melbourne Dr Mark Hobart Who Cared for Abandoned Elderly in 2020 Lockdown. 16 November. Available at https://marktaliano.net/help-melbourne-dr-mark-hobart-who-cared-for-abandoned-elderly-in-2020-lockdown. Accessed: 29 April, 2022.

The Defender Staff (2022) Young Man Sues Merck: Wants Accountability for Injuries Caused by Gardasil HPV Vaccine, 3 November. Available at https://childrenshealthdefense.org/defender-merrick-brunker-merck-lawsuit-gardasil-hpv-vaccine/

The Grandmothers Wisdom available at https://www.grandmotherswisdom.org.

The Highwire with Dell Bigtree (2022) Amish Farmer Facing Jail Time, 5 September. Available at https://podcasts.apple.com/us/podcast/the-amish-farmer-facing-jail-time/id1227863378?i=1000578422165. Accessed: 16 September, 2022.

The Intra-Body Nano Network Compilation, 6 September, 2023. Video credited to Unite For Truth Scotland. Available at https://odyssey.com@Watch The Spell:2/The-intra-body-nano-network-compilation.

The Perth Group (2017) HIV – a virus like no other, 12 July. Available at https://www.theperthgroup.com/HIV/TPGVirusLikeNoOther.pdf.

The Truth For Health Team (2022) A Bounty On a COVID Patient's Life Could Reach Half A Million, 14 September. Available at https://www.americaoutloud.com/the-bounty-a-patient's-life-could-reach-half-a-million.Accessed: 26 September, 2022.

Thomas, P (2024) The Vaxxed – Unvaxxed Data Presentation 18 October. Available at https://www.doctorsandscience.com/presentations.

Transcriber B (2022) The Peoples' convoy, a truckers freedom convoy from California to Washington DC, 23 February - 5 March, 2022. Available at https://web.archive.org/web/20220223003221/https://thepeoplesconvoy.org/.

Tsiang A, Havis M. Covid-19 Attributed Cases and Death are Statistically High in States and Countries with 5th Generation Millimeter Wave Wireless Telecommunications in the United States. Medical Research Archives, 12 April, 2021: https://doi.org/10.18103/mra.v9i4.2371.

Tyler Thompson, Laura-Lynn (2021) Doctor Andrew Kaufman, 6 August. Available at https://www.lauralynn.tv/2021/08/doctor-andrew-kaufman.html.

Tyler Thompson, Laura-Lynn, (2022) Attorney Reiner Fuellmich - Crimes Against Humanity Tour, 5 May. Available at https://www.lauralynn.tv/2022/05/attorney-reiner-fuellmich-crimes-against.html. Accessed: 18 May, 2022.

VAERS Summary for Covid-19 Vaccines Through 7/9/2021. Available at https://vaersanalysis.info/2021/07/16/vaers-summary-for-covid-19-vaccines-through-7-9-2021/

Vandersteel, A (2021) Judy Mikovits PhD. Antidote for Vaccine Toxin and Warns Against Dangerous Fake One, 15 November. Available at https://theplantstrongclub.org/2021/11/15/judy-mikovits-phd-antidote-for-vaccine-toxin-and-warns-against-dangerous-fake-one-forbiddenknowledgetv-net/ Accessed: 18 April, 2022.

Ventura, J (2010) Skyhorse Publishing, New York, USA.

Watt, K available at https://bailiwicknews.substack.com (Katherine Watt).

Wells, S D (2012) History of Medicine: The former Chairman of Bayer, maker of children's aspirin, was found guilty of Nazi crimes and sentenced to prison, 16 July. Available at naturalnews.com.

Wigington, D (2014) Climate Engineering Weather Warfare, and the Collapse of Civilization, 31 January. Available at https://www.geoengineeringwatch.org/climate-engineering-weather-warfare-and-the-collapse-of-civilization/

Wigington, D (2021) Graphene Skies, 29 July. Available at https://geoengineeringwatch.org/graphene-skies.

William Wallace quotes. Available at https://quotes.thefamouspeople.com/william-wallace-203.php.

Willingham, E (2015) A Congressman, a CDC Whistleblower and an Autism Tempest in a Trashcan, 6 August. Available at https//www.forbes.com/sites/emilywillingham/2015/08/06/a-congressman-a-cdc-whistleblower-and-an-autism-tempest-in-a-trashcan.

World Council for Health (2021) Dr Stephani Seneff: Covid-19 Vaccines and neurodegenerative Disease. Available at https://worldcouncilforhealth.org.

World Council for Health (2023) Why Professor Bhakdi's Court Ruling Will Empower the Great Reset, 25 May. Available at https://worldcouncilforhealth.org/news/blog/bhakdi-court-ruling/

World Doctors Alliance, available at https://worlddoctorsalliance.cm.

Zeee, M (2022) Interview With Dr Mark Hobart. Available at https://zeeemedia.com/interview/dr-mark-hobart-australian-health. Accessed: 3 May, 2022.

Zeee, M (2022) World Premiere: Conference of Conscience, Australian Doctors Finally Speak Out, Part 1, 19 May. Available at https://zeeemedia.com/interview/world-premiere-conference-of-conscience-australian-doctors-finally-speak-out-part-1/ Accessed: 19 July, 2022.

Zeee, M (2022) ZEROTIME - Political Hypocrisy & Scandal, Aussie Doctor Speaks Out About Shocking Vaxx Injuries, 31 August.

Available at https://zeeemedia.com/interview/zerotime-political-hypocrisy-scandal-aussie-doctor-speaks-out-about-shocking-vaxx-injuries/ Accessed: 2 September, 2022.

Zeee, M (2022) Interview with Aussie farmer Wade Northausen - Incoming Food Shortages, Population Starvation and The Fight of Our Lives, 2 September. Available at https://zeeemedia.com/interview/aussie-farmer-wade-northausen-incoming-food-shortages-population-starvation-the-fight-of-our-lives/ Accessed: 9 September, 2022.

Zeee, M (2022) Interview with Dr David Nixon, 25 October. Available at https://zeeemedia.com/interview/world-first-robotic-arms-assembling-via-nanotech-inside--covid-19-vaccines-filmed-in-real-time-david-nixon.

Zeee, M (2023) Capturing the Soul Through Technology, 10 May. Available at https://zeemedia.com/interview/maria-zeee-celeste-solum. Accessed: 18 May, 2023.

Zeee, M (2023) Interview with Hope & Tivon - WBAN: They Have Achieved the Transhumanism "System Upgrade", 22 November. Available at https://zeeemedia.com/interview/hope-tivon-they-have-achieved-the-transhumanism-system-upgrade

Zelenko, V available at https://vladilmirzelenkomd.com

BIBLIOGRAPHY

Children's Health Defense Team (2021) Study: Fewer Cases of Autism, Allergies in Unvaccinated Children, 25 June. Available at https://childrenshealthdefense.org/defender/fewer-cases-autism-allergies-unvaccinated-children/ Accessed: 28 May, 2022.

Daniel, I (2022) The Jerusalem Report available at https://live.childrenshealthdefense.org/shows/the-jerusalem-report.

Emoto, M (2003) The True Power of Water, Atria Books, New York.

Haich, E (1965) Initiation, George Allen and Unwin Ltd, London.

Hecht, E (2022) Pfizer Failed to Inform Us About These Vaccine Health Risks, 12 April. Available at https://dailyclout.io/pfizer-failed-to-inform-us-about-these-vaccine-health-risks/ Accessed, 20 April, 2022.

Integrative Pediatrics, The Dr Paul Approved Vaccine Plan. Available at https://www.integrativepediatrics.online.com/uploads//1/0/9/2/109222957/the-vaccine.

IOF, Prod (2012) Yet We Sow: Voices of Organic Farmers After Fukushima, (video file) available at www.youtube.com/watch?v=MPd7YPtiwo.

Kirsch, S (2023) Data from New Zealand Ministry of Health shows that the COVID vaccines have killed over 10 million worldwide, 1 December. Available at: https://kirschsubstack.com/p/data-from-us-medicare. Accessed: 8 December, 2023.

Latypova, S (2022) Independent Researchers Examining Pfizer mRNA Vaccines Strange Reports, 25 October. Available at https://www.trialsitenews.com/a/direct-microscopic-examination-

Leader, F (2023) Black Nobility 101, 12 August. Available at https://francesleader.substack.com/p/black-nobility-101.

Mawson A R, Ray B D, Bhuiyan A R, Jacob B. Published, 24 April, 2017, Pilot comparative study on the Health of vaccinated and unvaccinated 6-to-12-year-old US children: https://doi.org/10.15761/JTS.1000186.

Mihalcea, A (2022) "Shedding" - Understanding Self Spreading Vaccines in the Setting of Novel mRNA Technology, 30 June. Available at https://anamihalceamdphd.substack.com.

Mihalcea, A (2022) Irrefutable Proof of Self-Assembly Structures in C19 Shots - Time Lapsed Videos Show Microchip-like Structures Assembling and Disassembling - (updated video links), 26 October. Available at www.anamihalceamdphd.substack.com/.

Morning Star available at https://morningstaronline.co.uk/a-ca73-the-dark-history-of-bayer-chemicals.

National Vaccine Information Centre available at https://www.medalerts.org/vaersdb/index.php. Accessed: 28 May, 2022.

Natural News.com (2012) History of Medicine: The Former Chairman of Bayer, Makers of Children's Aspirin, was Found Guilty of War Crimes and Sentenced to Prison, 16 July. Available at https://www.naturalnews.com/036484-bayer-nazi-war-crimes.html.

Queensland Peoples' Protest available at: https://qpp.life.

Reid, D (1993) Guarding The Three Treasures, Simon & Schuster, London.

Sanders, B (2022) The American Crisis: A Country Divided Cannot Stand, 2 March. Available at https://thewisdomwarrior.com/bodhisanders/ Accessed: 1 July 2023.

Schlechtriem, M (2021) Vertical Farming: A Step Towards the Green Cities of the Future, 20 September. Available at https://www.meilirobots.com/resources-list/vertical-farming.

Siri, A (2022) Why a Judge Ordered FDA to Release Covid-19 Vaccine Data Pronto, 18 January. Available at https://news.bloomberglaw.com.

Young Global Leaders available at https://www.younggloballeaders.org.

www.ingramcontent.com/pod-product-compliance
Lightning Source LLC
Chambersburg PA
CBHW061726070526
44583CB00024B/3023